FRIENDSHIP WITH THOUGHT

Ronnie Jerome Dufeal

authorHOUSE®

AuthorHouse™ UK Ltd.
500 Avebury Boulevard
Central Milton Keynes, MK9 2BE
www.authorhouse.co.uk
Phone: 08001974150

First published by AuthorHouse 02/18/2011

ISBN: 978-1-4567-7479-0 (sc)
ISBN: 978-1-4567-7480-6 (e)

ABOUT THE BOOK

You like me want to be happy and to share your happiness with your loved ones. The natural laws and principles in this book are powerful for bringing about personal changes and at the same time easy to understand and easy to apply.

This Book is about a new way of thinking which is call Friendship with thought. The book contains life changing information. Because our feelings follow our thoughts this way of thinking puts you in the driving seat. It puts you in control of your feelings and in every situation you are, in. The book is direct and easy to understand. I have deliberately kept the paragraphs in small digestible bits so reading becomes easier.

In this book, you will find some new strange ways of thinking. At first, this may be frightening to you in a wonderful way. That is because as humans we are naturally cautious about the unknown. People usually stick to what they know even if it causes them pain. To change from pain to happiness you must change even if this may be fearful at the beginning. As you start to see clearly, you will become confident and fearless. Also included in this book is what, is call the Breath method. You can use

The Breath method to install and program in you whatever you choose to "be" and do.

The principle of Friendship with Thought as explained in the book is simple to understand and easy to apply in your life. It is so simple; keep it that way you can waste a lot of time making it more difficult. It will take a little effort to remind yourself of this principle however, that effort is well worth it. The knowledge contain in these pages has the wonderful, amazing power to enable you to do and have anything and everything you want and choose. This is not your everyday thinking you may be shocked. However when you get over your shock you will be amazed. You may at last realize that this is what you have been looking for all your life. Your power is in your thought.

ABOUT THE AUTHOR

Ronnie Dufeal graduated in the humanities from Guildhall University London. He has worked, in social care for most of his career and has a deep interest in how humans function. To better his understanding why people do what they do he has delved into physiology, philosophy and religion. He truly believes that humans are much more than they THINK they are. He also believes the knowledge he has discovered will be of value to others as much as they are to him. He believes that, this knowledge will change you for the better.

Contents

WELCOME

Welcome to the beginning of the rest of your happy, magical wonderful life. You are about to start a new wonderful happy journey. On this journey, you will discover certain things you suspected but just did not have the knowledge, the information to complete the picture until now. On this journey, you will discover certain things that will astonish you. You will be pleasantly surprise. Some of what, you will discover in these pages are shrouded in mystery. Some are; kept as secrets and some are illusion of our world. A mystery is no longer a mystery when you understand it. A secret is no longer a secret once it has been revelled. An illusion is no longer an illusion when you know it. The information in these pages will expose the illusion of everyday life.

You will be, introduce to the natural principle of Friendship with thought. By applying this principle, you will have the confidence and power to do things you need to do. You would not be scared nor would it be difficult or hard for you to do whatever you want to do. By applying Friendship with thought, you no longer have to fight to get what you want. You will take pleasure in doing what you want to do. Use these natural laws and principles to do and have anything you want. Being natural laws and principles they will not work for some and nor for others. They work for anyone who know about them and apply them in their life. They will work for you if you apply them in your life.

I guest by you choosing and reading, this book you are hoping to discover something of value to you. I promise you, you will be well pleased with the knowledge you are about to discover. The information in these pages is design to install in you indestructible self-beliefs. You will easily learn how to eliminate the crippling disease of self-doubt and all limitations that hold you back. The information will wake you up and train you to be mentally active. You will be, introduced to some new natural laws and principles. As you progress any old negative thought patterns you may have will be replace by new positive get up and go thoughts. Once your thoughts, has been reprogrammed you will naturally think like an optimist. Your outlook on life will change from predominantly negative to predominantly positive and you will get the results accordingly.

Your life will reflect you new frame of thinking. With a positive mindset, you will expect the best and you will naturally and easily, do things to have the best. With your new positive mindset, you will expect to succeed in what you do and you will. The natural laws and principles herein will help you handle any problem easily and quickly. You will see problems as challenges that you can easily handle because of the new way you think of them. What used to be difficult for you to do will become easy for you to do. When you implement these natural laws and principles, your life becomes easy. You may have been trying for years to understand or achieve certain things with little or no success, not anymore. You will come to, fully realize that everyone and everything involves thoughts. You will know that you can control your thoughts to give you anything you want. With your newfound knowledge, you will best be able to set your aims, your wonderful goals more precisely. Your new knowledge will motivate you to take action to have anything you want. Your new knowledge will give you the power to do.

In order for you to reap the benefits of this information, you need to be committed to your continuous self-improvements. If you recognize any negative traits in you, you must be willing to give them up. When you give up any negative trait, you will have changed that particular trait. A while ago, I heard a phrase concerning people who are dieting to lose weight. The person said the diet that worked for them is the one they stock too. To have the things you want in your life you have to change you. To change you must be committed to your changes. You must stick to your program of change until you know that you have changed. You create your life with your attitude. You tell yourself what to think and do which create your life as it is. You must be willing to change your attitude and your personality. If you continue with your old attitude and personality, which is not getting you the things you want you will get more of the same, the things

3

you do not want. Yes, you need to change the whole of you, when you do the excitement starts.

There is an old saying that knowledge is power. Use the information herein to change you. When you experience the information herein, you will know you have the priceless knowledge to do anything you want.. Here are some ways in which your life would be transform if you use the information contain in this book. You will have an abundance of material things. Your life will be completely different, for the better. You will have the best because you will know that you can easily have the best. Why go second-class when you can just as easily go first class? Your health will dramatically improve including your appearance and any weigh lost you desire. You will be a happier person with knowledge and wisdom. You will be a magnet for other people seeking advice and friendship. You will become even more loving to yourself and more compassionate to others. By reading this, book you will realize and find out many things you can easily do. This book will open new ways to create your new reality.

WHAT IF YOU KNOW?

What if, you know that everything is all right and that, everything is going to be all right? How will you act? What will you do? What if the condition of your visit to earth is you take nothing with you? That you remember; no pass experience. That you are here for, the experience of it. That you create your, own experiences with your thoughts. And that you deliberately chose what type of human you would become. How will this knowledge make you act? How will you feel? What will you do? What, if nothing can go wrong? What, if there is no right or wrong unless you think it so? What if the, purpose of being here on earth as a human is not to serve others, society or some cause but to fully experience the most precious most important value in the universe THOUGHT? Everyone and everything springs from thought. What if you, are here to experience your own conscious self with increasing peace, prosperity, joy, love, luxury and happiness? The primary responsibility of thought is to preserve itself.

What, if you know that you are who you are because of your thoughts? And you have and do all you have and do because of your thoughts, your feelings, your choices and your time. If you knew with absolute certainty that you are who you are, you do what you do, and you have all that you have. Because of applying these four qualities either consciously or subconsciously in your life and either way you get the results. How would you feel? What will you do? What will you change?

What if no matter what everything is now O.K.? What if no matter what everything will be O.K.? What will you choose to do and be? What if you; were absolutely, certain that everything that exists, is thought, manifested? Thought experiencing, itself in countless billions of various forms? If you knew, that you are thought manifested and experiencing it-self as you? What will be your predominant thoughts? What will be your way of life? If you knew; that you are pure conscious heavenly energy manifested as a human? How would you feel? By heavenly I mean nonphysical and yet is, real. Everything and everyone in existence or that have ever existed or will come into existence starts with thought. We contribute; give our predominant thoughts in various forms to the world and people. If you knew, that the things you say and do were making a positive difference, transforming people lives for the better. What would you do or say. We live in an intelligent universe. Look around and you will see design in everything including yourself. Everyone and everything are thoughts manifested in various forms.

Sometimes I will refer to thoughts as a single entity, as THOUGHT. I encourage you to see thought as a single entity that has manifested in billions of various ways. Realize that thought is limitless and is alive.

Thought is nonphysical and yet you know it exists. Everything that exists is energy in one form or another. Thought is energy manifested in countless various forms. In time all energy changes. What if death, is simply a change from one form of energy to another? What if death, makes it O.K. no matter what? What if death, brings you back to your pure energy form, your true essence? Knowing overcomes fear. Those who truly know thought intimately have no fear. Knowing that you have the most powerful energy in existence on your side will render all fears powerless. Especially so when you come to understand and accept that you are a part of that tremendous powerful energy. Yes, every man woman and child is part of that power you have within you. That powerful energy, that makes you who you are, is a part of everyone else. If you know everything is O.K., would you still be afraid? If you know everything is going to be O.K., would you still worry?

When you know with absolute certainty that thought is the master of the universe you will put full trust in yourself because you have that power within you. If you do not know your grate power you will be frighten of you. Some people are, fortunate enough to receive this knowledge this power. This is because of their honest searching for personal power. Some people are afraid to accept their great power. Some are afraid, to embrace what they recognize deep down, but are unfamiliar with. Knowledge builds trust, hope, confidence and faith in someone or something that you know well. We put our trust, hope and confidence in someone or something according to their qualities and abilities. If you do not know, someone or something you are likely to be afraid of them. With appropriate information, you are more likely to take appropriate action. You will not cross a rope bridge that span a dangerous deep gorge that is design to hold the weight of a person that weighs 100 lbs if you weigh 250 lbs. You will be afraid because you know the ability of the bridge is not up to standard.

If you knew that that bridge was design to hold a weight of 1100 lbs and you weigh only 250 lbs you will cross with confident. Because you know that, the bridge has the capacity to hold much more than your weight. Similarly, when you come to know that thought is limitless and you are a part of thought manifested. You will be, more friendly to thought in general. Once you know, that thought is your genie and is here to serve you, as you wish you would get used to controlling your thought better. You will come to put full confidence in your thoughts to achieve whatever you choose. When you control your thoughts, you control your life. Control of your life results in peace, prosperity and happiness. Your thoughts are real. They exist in the spiritual world or nonmaterial world as some people call it. Moreover, they can be manifested in the material world if you so choose.

Take a few seconds and look around you and you will soon become aware that everything around you is a thought that someone has bring into objective reality. Thought is a powerful intelligent energy responsible for all existence. Once you have unpicked the limitless power and potential of positive thoughts. You will gain unbeatable power over every situation or event, which touches your life. With your new powers you can have unlimited peace, prosperity, happiness and whatever else you choose forever. People who are not aware of the great power and potential of continuous positive thoughts will remain unaware and dissatisfied with almost everything. Including people and things which; are not parts of their life. People who are unaware of the limitless power of positive thought will continue to experience hardship and strife on earth. They are creating their hardship without fully realizing that they are the one who is doing so. Without realizing that, they are the ones who are creating their hardship they will blame others for not getting what they want.

Not realizing the, potential they have within them they will use thoughts predominantly negatively to create their experiences. They create predominant negative distractive unhappy way of living. They will succumb to their predominant negative way of thinking which their life will reflect. It can be different. By positive, I mean happy thoughts, feelings and action. By negative, I mean sad or unhappy thoughts, feelings and behaviour. Positive thoughts are the energy of life, pleasure and abundance. Negative thoughts are the energy of pain and destruction. Consciously or subconsciously from these two poles we make our choices and get the results accordingly.

Everything you do you have learned, likewise you will have to learn to control your thoughts to achieve whatever you want. It's, like having the most beautiful car in the world but not being able to drive. If you cannot, drive you will have to rely on other people to get you where you want to go and that can be most inconvenient. You may also not be making full use of your beautiful car. In order to make the most of your wonderful possession you will have to learn to drive. You have to learn to control your lovely car. It's the same with your glorious powerful thought. You need to learn to be in total control to feel and do as you please. Realise that everything in existence came about through thought, if not yours then someone else's. You have the same quality of thought in you as everyone else.

What if you, know with absolute certainty that you are here just for the experience of it? That everyone and everything you think of triggers either, positively or negatively feelings in you. All because of what you think of them or it? What will your; predominant thoughts of people and things be, if you knew this to be true? What if you knew it is all a matter of choice, your choice? If you know, that you have total control of what you choose to think and do. What would you think? What would you do? How will you act? If you knew that fear, is a feeling cause by what you are thinking, about? What would you choose to think, about?

If you knew for sure that confidence, prosperity and happiness are feelings caused by what or who you are thinking about? What or who, will you make your predominant thoughts? What would you make your regular thoughts about people and things? Would you choose to think continuous positive thoughts? If pleasant thoughts; of people and things mean confidence, happiness and prosperity for you? What type of thoughts would you habitually think about people and things? If you; knew that happiness could only be, found in you how would you feel? If you knew, that happiness is, made up of positive thoughts and feelings about people or things, what would you make your dominant thoughts? How would you feel about making continuous positive thoughts your way of life? How would you, feel and what will you think if you knew that happiness is a state of mind, a state of being? Would you be, more selective about what and who you think about.

During your day do your best to think about someone or something that you like. Do something that you like. Continually give yourself those lovely thoughts and feelings. When you do, you will have started an upward spiral of positive energy. Do your best to think and see most people and things as nice. We live in a limitless world. If you want something or to do something the fact that you have not done it nor have it yet does not mean that, it is impossible for you to do or have. If it is possible that means that you can have it or do it. Your thoughts make up your feelings. Therefore as you think, so you will also feel. Your feelings are the energy that drives you; you behave according to your feelings. It is well, known that the way people behave they get the results accordingly.

What we call good pleasant behaviour brings good pleasant results. What we call bad disruptive destructive behaviour brings similar results. People want to feel secure, happy and peaceful. Bad behaviour brings bad results that people do not want. Do your best to, regularly be aware of what you are thinking because what you are thinking determines how you feel. How you feel determines your action. Your action or reaction determines the results you get. The result you get determines what you think and feel your mood. Have something nice to change your mood. Flowers work they change people's mood, they cheer us up. When you honestly think you look good you will feel good.

The fact that you are alive means that you must be somewhere thinking and doing something. Is what you are thinking making you feel happy? Is what you are doing making you happy? Only you can honestly answer those, question for you. If what you, are thinking or doing is not making you feel happy you are free to change your thoughts and actions. Today is a good day. Each day do your best to have something good to look forward too. If you regularly do things that make you happy, you will have more happy memories. You were; made to be happy you are worthy it. Your happy memories are dependent on your happy thoughts and actions you take today. The happy things you do today will be your happy memories in your future.

YOUR WEALTH FRIENDSHIP WITH THOUGHT

Welcome to Friendship with thought. I would like to introduce you to a magical philosophy called, Friendship with thought. Friendship with thought is a way of thinking that will result in you having everything you have ever dreamed of and more. Friendship with thought is **you think of and see your-self, people and things as thoughts manifested.** YOU THINK OF EVERYONE AND EVERYTHING AS THOUGHTS MANIFESTED, INCLUDING YOURSELF. By thinking this, way you are consciously linking positive thought to people and things. This way of thinking will open your eyes to a new reality. This way of thinking enables you to see yourself, people and things as being, connected to each other. Thoughts are energy.

The world is made up of, the energy of thoughts that has been manifested in objective reality. By thinking and seeing the world this way you will become confidence and fearless in whatever you want to do. By thinking this way you can prosper anywhere on earth in any situation or condition. To realize your dreams, your new powerful prosperous new way of life, you need to make some changes.

You must be willing and make a commitment to yourself to change your personality and attitude with regards, to how you see yourself and life. A commitment is something you can give and do for yourself. A commitment is deciding once, and for all never to go back to your old ways of thinking and of seeing people and things. Your commitment to yourself involve, developing your new personality and new attitude. Your commitment include, developing a new way of thinking and of seeing the world. For only when you commit to your change, you will do things to change. You can achieve fantastic things in your life; however, you must want to achieve fantastic things in your life. To start achieving fantastic things in your life you need to change your old ways of thinking. If you do not change, you will continue to do and to get the same things in your life.

You need to, habitually think mainly positive things about yourself, people and things. You need to develop continuous positive thoughts about you. Everyone and everything that exist is a result of thought. Friendship with thought not only show you how to create positive thoughts, it automatically creates positive thoughts as you think of what it is. The philosophy of Friendship with thought applies to all possible situations you could or will ever find yourself. Friendship with thought is a method for winning limitless advantage anywhere and anytime you choose by being in control of your thoughts.

Friendship with thought requires a new integrated way of thinking which generates a certain vibrational frequencies. This in turn creates positive situations and events to your advantage. Your positive thoughts and feelings are your inner power, your inner strength; your inner energy to do anything, you want to do. Realise that your inner thoughts and feelings are your inner person, your inner life. Your inner life reflects your outer life your life in objective reality. How strong is your inner person? How powerful is your inner person? How much energy has your inner life got? Using Friendship with thought, you can have as much energy as you desire. With continuous positive thoughts, you can be as powerful as you wish. With continuous positive thoughts, you can be as strong as you want. With continuous positive, thought you can do anything you want and have as much money as you choose. I will remind, you that Friendship with thought is, a way of thinking, it's a way of thinking and seeing people and things as thought manifested in various forms.

Think of thought as a single entity that has manifested itself in countless billions of ways. When you look around you will soon realize that everyone and everything are thoughts manifested. Those manifestations are, made possible by thought manifesting itself in countless forms. When you create something, you are manifesting your thoughts. You had to; first think about whatever you made then you made it. Even if you just made it as you were going along you still had to do some thinking, even if that thinking was for a short while. You thought about if first before you made it. Thus thought, manifesting, itself. You are a thought manifesting a thought. Thus thought, manifesting thought. By applying Friendship with thought in your life you will notice every day you life is getting better.

Friendship with thought gives you all the power you need to make your life exactly as you choose. This means that you are always in a winning situation. Once you understand and apply the principles of Friendship with thought, you can control your thoughts and every situation you are in. By positively seeing people and things as thoughts manifested. You will be controlling your thought, as you do you will become a leader. Leaders are always in control that is what makes them leaders. I am here talking about front leaders, what you see is what you get type of leader. I am not talking about someone else pulling the strings behind the scene. I am talking about real power in the hands of whom you see as leader in control.

Friendship with thought is natural and can be applied anywhere anytime to anything in life. To achieve your dreams set yourself challenges and assignments that will bring you closer to them. Use Friendship with thought to carry out the challenges and assignments that you have set yourself without; delay. All over the, world people are doing their best to avoid pain. By applying Friendship with thought, you will find your assignments and challenges much easier and painless to do.

You can have immediate positive results by applying Friendship with thought in objective reality. The reason for those immediate results is that your state of mind depends on your thoughts. Ideas are thoughts, bullets cannot kill an idea, nor could swords kill ideas. You only have to look in science, politic or in the religious world to realize this fact. Thousands of years, ago men and women have developed ideas that are still being use today. Ideas that, are relevant today as they were back then. Yes, some thoughts are still alive after thousands of years. Thoughts will always be; we will always have ideas. People can kill an idea only by hiding it, by keeping it secret, by not repeating it. Come to realize that "Thought" is the energy of creation and the energy of destruction. Positive thoughts create and negative thoughts destroy.

Friendship with thought is a way of thinking and being; a state of being that generates confidence and removes all limitations. There is an; old Chinese saying that say; what is inside of you that is what matters. What thoughts do you have inside of you? How much do you value your thoughts? How useful is your ability to create your own thoughts? You become an automatic winner when you use Friendship with thought way of thinking in all areas of your life. Even if your situation is low at present, you can reverse it by applying this information. Friendship with thought will lift your spirit to do anything you choose. You can only benefit yourself by breaking free of limiting negative thoughts. By seeing people and things as thoughts, you automatically think of them as parts of you. You are no longer frightened of people or situations when you know for certain, that they are extensions of you.

With; Friendship with thought in operation in your life, you can totally take control of your future. When you control your thoughts, you control your life. You can control your thoughts. Therefore, you can control; your situations and whatever come to you. You can be a person with a new personality and new attitude who generates predominately, pure positive thoughts and feelings about people and things. You never again have to feel unhappy or incompetent in any situation. You can use Friendship with thought knowledge to gain in any personal relationship or any other situation. For any friendship to grow people, need to accept the personality and attitude of each other in that relationship.

Once you get used to using Friendship with thought you will be a friend of thought your positive thoughts will protect you. You will never again, be taken advantage of. Your natural happy feel good positive thoughts you generate will protects you in all situations. You never again have to depend on anything or anyone outside your-self. Either for happiness or anything else because you know that happiness and everyone and everything is thoughts manifested. The situation you are in is a thought you can control. Not many people are consciously in control of their habitual thoughts. People who are in control of their habitual thoughts are all leaders. These people take control of businesses, politics and religion. They are usually happy and prosperous people.

Everyone wants to feel happy, make people happy and they will drop their defensive guard and leave you in control. They will hand over control to you because you make them feel happy. Yes, remember that you can control your thoughts.

The knowledge and application of Friendship with thought will fascinate you to the point of change. You will be intrigue by this new way of thinking. Friendship with thought way of thinking feels good. When you have adopted this new natural, way of thinking you will see people and things in a new light. Everything comes to you by way of your thoughts. You will find life much easier and more rewarding. You will learn many things about yourself you never thought possible. This I promise you. When you become aware, that everyone and everything in our world are thoughts. I guarantee you will be amazed, fascinated and flabbergasted all at the same time when you see through the illusions of our world.

When you realize that, everyone and everything are thoughts manifested in objective reality. Everyone and everything came about because of thoughts. Your thoughts are real and exist in the realms of thoughts, in the realm of all possibilities. If your thoughts were not real, they would not affect you the way they do. Your thoughts not only affect you but they also affect other people and things. Something that is not real could never have had such effect on our planet. Your thoughts exist as pure nonmaterial energy. However, on a deeper level you know this knowledge to be true. Anything that fascinates you; you will give your time and attention to and you will get more of the same. When you are, fascinated by someone or something all thoughts break their bounds.

When you are fascinated, dormant energy starts moving as if by magic. You find yourself with extra energy and power to do wonderful things in line with what you are, fascinated by. You will find energy that you never thought possible for you. In your state of fascination, you discover a new you where the impossible becomes possible. Once your negative thought has been broken, your limitless positive thoughts come into play. With your positive thoughts at full swing, your awareness is at its peak. And you find yourself in a new amazing and wonderful state of positive attraction. When you habitually think, everything is going your way you will attract more of the same. You can use anyone that annoy you to practice being patience. You need to develop a strong feeling of desire for what you want. You will also need to develop patience in order to get what you want. Everything you know you have learned. You can learn to be even more patient than you are at present. People learn from others to do things in various ways. To learn to do new things we need to associate with different people.

Friendship with thought will show you and help you develop your strong desires.

YOUR THOUGHTS CAN SERVE YOU AS A STIMULUS OR THEY CAN SERVE AS A SEDATIVE. If you use your thoughts as a sedative, you would not do what you need to do when you suppose to do it. Whenever you have something, you want to do but find you do not have the emotional energy to get on with it notice what you are thinking. It is likely that you are thinking something negative about the object of your attention. If you are thinking something negative, you are using your thoughts as a sedative. To use your thoughts as a stimulus think positive thoughts about whatever you want to do and you will create the energy to do. With the energy to do you will do what you want to do. You need to get use to this way of thinking. Once you have made this way of thinking your own you will naturally have the energy to "do".

As you progress, if you have read something in these, pages that amazes you. Just stop for a few second and look around and you will have confirmation for yourself that it is so. Yes, it is true. This knowledge is all around you already you just did not connected the dots until now. As you go through this book, I will remind you of the concept behind Friendship with thought. These reminders will make it easier for you to understand and apply this information in your everyday life. You can change. If you are, not satisfied with the life you are living you need to change. If you do, not change you will continue to do the same things and you will continue to get the same results. The best way to change and keep those changes is to be committed to changes in your thoughts about people and things. This commitment to your change of thoughts will result in changes in your lifestyle. This includes your health, money and doing things differently.

Realize that you can create the energy to accomplish anything you want. The same energy that was use to create the universe is the same energy you use every day to do whatever you want to do. Yes anytime you want to do something you need to create the will to do, the energy to do, the power to do. Without this energy, you would not do what you want to do. Without this energy, you would not get far. You create this energy with your positive thoughts about the things you want and need to do. When you feel, excited about doing certain things you are creating the energy to do. When you have created, the energy to do you will have the will to do and you will do anything you want. The stronger your will to do is the sooner you will do what you choose to do. Your knowledge will completely change your life for the better. We all have different experiences in life. You exist as you with your unique individual experiences, which only you have created and are experiencing.

According to your old beliefs, you may become excited and afraid at the same time at the information contained within these pages. People are usually afraid of what they do not understand. Upon understanding this, information your happiness will blossom. If its happiness, you are looking for read on. If its peace and prosperity, you are looking for read on. If its freedom, you are looking for then read on. Welcome. You can use Friendship with thought to increase your happiness and wealth now and in the future for as long as you choose.

TO EXPERIENCE LIFE DIFFERENTLY YOU MUST CHANGE, YOU MUST CHANGE YOUR PERSONALITY AND ATTITUDE. Friendship with thought principles is the way forward for anyone who is seeking change of personality and attitude. By adopting this new natural way of thinking about people and things, you will change. You can easily make happiness and limitless prosperity your predominant way of life. Friendship with thought is a positive thought making method. It is a way that guides anyone who chooses to implement it in their life to create peace, prosperity and happiness. You can be who you want to be by using your continuous positive thoughts. The concepts of Friendship with thought allow you to summon pure positive thoughts for help in any situation. This help will result in control, power, prosperity and happiness. All you have to do is think of and see people and things as thoughts manifested that have created your present situation. The more you practice seeing the world like this is the more happiness and prosperity will come to you. Have you notice that we usually like those who like us. We like each other only because of what we think about each other.

Friendship with thought includes a concept that lets you know what you are thinking and how you are feeling in any situation. Importantly Friendship with thought tells you what to do to gain an advantage in that situation. Remember that you are always in a situation so Friendship with thought can help in every moment of your life. Your new positive frame of mind will nullify any negative fearful or painful thought in all situations. This fearless state leaves you in control to take the lead. The power to "do" must come from you, from within you and this is exactly what Friendship with thought does. Friendship with thought thoughts lets you create unbeatable power within you in any situation. With this power, you easily take control and "do" to win. Fearless people are happy people because that is what fearlessness produce, happiness. Fearless people see positive potential in situations that fearful people would not see. Keep in mind that we see what we expect to see.

You need to be very careful that you are not very dependent on others in almost all areas of your life. You need to fulfil your potential yourself. This means that, you need to become independent, emotionally, financially and intellectually. You know what, you need to do, do not leave what you need to do for yourself to others to do. If you leave, what you need to do for yourself to others you are likely to be disappointed. If you are, disappointed because you do not have what you want because of leaving it to others you will blame others for what you do not get. We become happier and more prosperous by providing competitive value for others. To feel of value, to experience your potential, to be happy and to prosper you need to take action. If you are, frighten about taking action. Keep in mind that fear is just your negative thoughts about a person or thing. Usually fears are based on what if's.

When you learn to, habitually and consistently think Friendship with thought thoughts. You automatically create situations that deliver confidence, peace prosperity, happiness and love to you and others. By understanding the principle of Friendship with thought and using it, you become a winner. You will experience greater pleasures, greater happiness, with guaranteed peace, prosperity and joy for life. Because it is, these types of qualities that create your wonderful situations that follow each other as one long wonderful life situation. This magical state becomes your way of life, your natural state of being. By using Friendship with thought, you can create your magical situations for life.

For as long as you make Friendship with thought your way of life, thinking and seeing people as wonderful thoughts manifested in various ways. You will create situations that deliver all you have ever dreamed of and more. Look carefully and you will discover that all there is are thoughts manifested in countless ways. Thought, Happiness, love, pleasure, joy and laughter has no limits. You will create situations that attract to you people and things that trigger those wonderful feelings in you. You can only create positive or negative situations. Always be aware of the situation you are creating by what you are thinking saying and doing. If what you, are thinking or doing does not feel good change it. Change your thoughts and what you are, doing.

Everything has to be, maintained in good condition if they are to serve their purpose. Likewise if you are to keep those wonderful people and things your situation must be, maintained. Maintain your thought of seeing people and things as wonderful thought manifested in various ways. Yes, you must maintain your habitual thought of thinking and seeing people and things as wonderful thoughts. Thoughts that has been, manifested in various forms. This way of thinking and seeing life leads to life and happiness. If you stop, thinking that way. You will automatically stop creating pure positive situations where you are in control. You will disconnect yourself from Friendship with thought. And will revert to a poverty and painful way of thinking which is a destructive way of life. You have the power to create any situation you choose. The essence, the core of life is Pure thought.

Thought is energy, express in billions of different ways, in billions of various forms. Conscious thought can control nature the present and what-ever the future bring. We all must do our very best and resist negativity by putting forth necessary positive thoughts and effort. It is the only way to make your world as you choose it to be. People who stop who surrender to negativity because of laziness will allow negativity to take over their lives. They will create situations accordingly. Such people would not get the happiness they are looking for.

Negativity and laziness do not result in prosperity and happiness. If the above, applies to you as they were applicable to me some years ago then you have a second chance I encourage you to take it. Included in this book is a natural, simple and powerful method to install in you programs of happiness and prosperity. As you start to use it, you will notice immediate happy changes in your feelings. This method is call The Breath method. You can use The Breath method and Friendship with thought to create pure positive thoughts. By using these, methods you will create action based on what you think and feel. Friendship with thought allows people to avoid the automatic control of negative thoughts. If you do not deliberately, choose positive thoughts that motivate you. Then you are, left with only one choice that automatically create negative thoughts and act accordingly.

Positivity has to be, created with effort and be, maintained. Using Friendship with thought, with practice you do not think about the good and bad of people and things. You automatically see all people and things as thoughts, which are all extensions of you. That is why Friendship with thought is so important, you automatically see everyone and everything as thoughts manifested in various forms. When something is, fun and easy people want to be part of it. That is what Friendship with thought does to life. It makes life easy and fun. As long as you are alive, you have to take part in life that is the very nature of life. Therefore, you might as well make it fun, you will enjoy it much more when you make it fun.

You are now taking in knowledge of how to make it fun. You have the tool, Friendship with thought, use it to gain advantage in every area of your life to have what you want and choose. When you; hear someone talking you automatically know to yourself that it is thought expressing itself. Because that is exactly what they are a thought expressing thoughts. When you see your surroundings, you automatically see thoughts manifested in countless various forms. Keep on using Friendship with thought on a daily basis and you will soon get used to experiencing life that way. A, whole new completely wonderful world will have opened to you. You will naturally want to hold onto your day because you are enjoying it so much. AT THE SAME TIME, YOU WILL LOOK FORWARD TO TOMORROW AND ALL THOSE WONDERFUL THOUGHTS YOU WILL EXPERIENCE. Keep in mind that life is one long experience and you experience it as you make it. Either consciously or subconsciously, you create your own experiences. Either, deliberately or unwittingly, you have created and will continue to create all your experiences.

When you consciously and deliberately create your own happy experiences then life becomes magical. Because you will create situations that, results in prosperity. You will ultimately prosper with the habitual use of Friendship with thought. People who decide not to use Friendship with thought will continue to think as usual and get the same results. They will continue to live a life of lack and fear and wonder why. It is no wonder because that is what their thoughts are predominantly producing. Their thoughts manifest themselves in the forms of situations, people and things in their lives. Our situations and experiences are reflections of our thoughts. Friendship with thought; creates only positive thoughts. By applying Friendship with thought in your life your predominant thoughts, moods and states will be predominantly happy. Happiness is exactly, what will be reflected in all areas of your life, yes happiness and well-being.

Your thoughts create your interpretations of your situations. You can create successful situations and interpretations accordingly. Successful situations lead to whatever you choose to have as part of your life. Negativity in all situations if not corrected will result in stagnation and death. Positivity in all situations results in growth and life. Positive feelings tell you that you are happy. Negative feelings are also valuable they tell you that you are thinking something negative and need to change your thoughts or situation. If left unattended your negative state will undermine your happiness, peace, prosperity and well-being. When you are habitually in positive situations, you will automatically be happy, cheerful and prosperous. In happy situations, people produce value for others, which results in value for themselves. People who live with Friendship with thought are positive, productive happy and exciting to be with. They live happy, prosperous meaningful lives. Anyone can at anytime choose to apply Friendship with thought in his or her life. Most people are usually afraid of doing. They are afraid of not being right so they stop trying after a short time.

For some people it feels much better not to try than to try and not succeed. If you stop, trying because of the fear of the pain of failure. Then you are deliberately limiting yourself of the wonders this world have to offer. You are stopping yourself all because of what you are thinking. Notice what you are thinking whenever you are afraid. You will soon discover that you are reflecting your fearful negative thoughts about a person, thing or situation. Friendship with thought will help get rid of those fears. For a happy prosperous life, you must choose to exert the effort to habitually think and see people and things as thought manifested in various ways. By thinking this way, you will lose all negative fears of people and things. You will know that you also are a thought manifested. Your thoughts are responsible for everything you do or have in your life. You are in control of your thoughts. You are responsible for your thoughts.

With this knowledge, you will no longer be afraid. You will start doing happy productive things. These happy productive things will create your situations and experiences accordingly. By you losing all fears, I mean that you will lose all negative fear of saying and doing that, which will make you prosperous.

Once you have created positive new thoughts about people and things you will automatically think and see people as part of you. You will no longer be afraid of your thoughts or of people and things including not being afraid of doing. Remember, sooner or later you must do. By applying Friendship with thought, you will create the energy necessary to do whatever you want, choose or desire to do.

The more confidently, positively and happily you do is the happier and more prosperous you will become. Friendship with thought creates positive situations, which help people to live peacefully, prosperously, calm, relax and happy lives. Having Friendship with thought in you, people will want to be with you. People will sense that they will benefit from being with you. You will benefit all involve with you; this will enable you to automatically benefit yourself. Friendship with thought thinkers experience life with ever-increasing joy, happiness and zest. Friendship with thought thinkers, welcome and embrace any effort to produce value for others, value which others want. People usually want to be happy. Happiness is a state of being, your happiness involve your positive thoughts and wonderful feelings. Your happiness is a reflection of your thoughts. The more happy, people and things you have to recall is the happier you will be.

You can use association of ideas to recall happiness to you. Where-by remembering one thing, it will automatically remind you of someone or something. By consciously associating good feelings to certain people and things every time you think of those people or things they will trigger happiness in you. That is how you formed your happiness in the first place, only you most likely did this subconsciously. Now you can consciously associate as much people and things to trigger happiness in you as you please. For example let us say you want to associate happiness to someone you love. Using the breath method, you mention the name of the person and look at the sky a split second after you mention their name. You do that fifty times during your day. You can split it up or you can do it all at once. You will find that any time you look at the sky in the future you will recall that person that makes you feel happy. According to research, the subconscious associate the number fifty with strong recall.

To be predominantly happy you must have continuous positive thoughts. You need to practice it for it to become a habit. You have to practice continuous positive thoughts for continuous positive thoughts to become habits of yours. All growth, all life are products, are results of continuous thoughts from various people. Once you have, mastered continuous positive thoughts the sky is your limit. By the time you finish reading this book you would have come to know with certainty that you deserve to live your life to the full. What I mean by this statement is; you deserve the best of everything good. If you are not having the best, someone else is having it. Someone has to have the best why not you. Do you think that you do not deserve the best? Do you think that the best is, reserved for someone else? The best is there for those who think that they deserve the best and have the confidence and power to go for the best.

The best belong to people like you who known that they can have the best when they think and feel they deserve the best. When you habitually think and feel you deserve the best, you will automatically expect the best and you will do things to get the best. With continuous positive thoughts, you can achieve anything. With continuous positive thoughts, you have no limit. Use Friendship with thought to create your continuous positive thoughts. You can also use The Breath Method to create habitual continuous positive thoughts. Patience and practice is the key to success. There is a time to say and there is a time to say little. Enjoy whoever or whatever you have as part of your life. Remember that whatever you do, as a human there will be a last time.

There will be a final time so enjoy and be happy with the people and things you have as part of your life. That is why you have them so be happy with them and enjoy them. Anything you honestly want to do search, you will find a way to do it. Your journey of discovery never stop's that is why it's so valuable, that's why it's so wonderful. Do your best to see positive qualities in people and things. Especially so in those people and things with whom, you have regular contact. If you practice seeing people and things in a positive light, it will soon become your natural way of seeing them. Keep in mind that you have found the master key that opens all doors to your happy prosperous life. That important key is, thought. Whenever you doubt yourself, you generate negative energy. People become afraid when they generate negative energy.

People lose their confidence when they think they are incapable or unsure of someone or something. Learn how to conquer your fears and you automatically learn how to succeed in whatever you choose. We create what we habitually think. If your thoughts are mainly about prosperity, that is exactly what you are programming in you. The opposite is also true. If your, habitually thoughts are of poverty that is what you are creating as part of your life. Believe that you will have plenty of the good things of life. Believe that you will be rich and you will become rich, you will do things to become rich. Your beliefs will take you there. By implementing, the methods as explained in these pages you will create a constant continuous state of prosperity and abundance. Once your flow, of prosperity get going it will not stop unless you stop it with negativity. So keep those positive thoughts and actions alive. Because of the law of duality feelings fade, this fact means from time to time you will be in a low mood. Think and do things to get out of that low mood as soon as possible. Whatever you do or say always do it or say it with a good motive. Always let your intentions, be good and pure. Notice how easy, it is to do something that makes you happy and how rewarding it feels once, you have done it.

Genuine; power and wealth are made possible through pure positive thoughts and action. Yes effort in needed to implement your thoughts. In order to implement your thoughts you will need the power of courage, confidence and self-belief. You will need the power of doing. That which you are about to do to make you happy you can do. By putting your positive productive thoughts into practice, you are in fact creating situations to gain the widest possible range of prosperity and happiness. Friendship with thought delivers powerful unbeatable advantages for all who choose to use it. People who live by creating pure positive thoughts habitually automatically create situations accordingly which delivers accordingly.

Every day find something wonderful about you, yes every day find something to be proud of yourself. Every day do something so you can say to yourself, I did well today I am proud of myself. This is like, giving your-self a pat on the back and saying well done. The sense of accomplishments gives natural highs with no side effects. The service of others brings all sorts of benefits including freedom. If you are focused on others well-being you are free from any fear that may hinder you. Concern for others, takes away the fears and leave you free to deliver happiness to others.

People become winners because they know how to win by having the power to "DO." They do things so they can win. If you do, not do something nothing will not happen. By putting Friendship with thought concept to work in your life you will have an invincible powerful tool. Use Friendship with thought to help you to do whatever you want to do. Use this tool to eradicate all negativities about yourself and your abilities. You need faith, trust and confidence in yourself to do what is necessary to solve all your problems. By becoming confident, you set yourself on the path to become a happy productive human. People have the personal responsibility to overcome speaking negative words. In order to live a positive prosperous and happy life we all need to overcome the urge to use negative words. This responsibility to speak positive up lifting words is a job that cannot be pass on to anyone else.

If we do not use negative words then, that leaves only positive up lifting words. People get used to negativity as a way of life, sad, as it is this is true. People easily become comfortable with unwanted situations. Consequently, their life is fill with predominantly negative thoughts about their unwanted situations. If people relinquishes, their responsibilities to produce competitive value for others they are in effect surrendering their life. When you produce, competitive value for others you automatically produce value for you. People surrender their life by asking others to produce competitive values for them. They ask others to solve their problems for them so they can become happy. We all have the ability and capacity to solve our problems. THE ONLY THING THAT IS STOPPING YOU FROM SOLVING YOUR OWN PROBLEMS IS NEGATIVITY IN THE FORM OF FEAR.

Some people think that solving their problems is too hard to solve, that solving their problems are beyond them. Notice what I have said, your problems, not someone else's problems, your problems that you are quite capable of solving. Let people solve their own problems, why should you be burden with someone else's problems. Problems are basically, things we have to do which we find difficult to do for various reasons. It all depends on what you think about your problems. If you are afraid of your problems, this fear will hinder you from doing things to solve them. You need the confidence to approach your problems without fear. When you have to do things, do what you find easy first before attempting to do something more difficult. You can do it if you think you can. You can do it if you believe you can.

Use Friendship with thought to build your confidence and you will do anything you want and choose to do. You will know for certain, and be convinced that your problems are freighting you only because of the negative thoughts you are thinking about them. You will no longer be afraid of doing what you want to do when you think positive things about them. You will discover that you are frightened only of your thoughts.

If you do not have, the information or knowledge to solve your problems this could be a problem in itself. All that is, needed in this case is the acquisition of information and knowledge in relation to your problem. Then apply that information and knowledge to your problem.

Thought is limitless you cannot run out of thoughts. What's more, you create your thoughts yourself. You control your thoughts. Your thoughts will trigger certain feelings in you. These feelings will either help you or hinder you accordingly. If your thoughts are positive they will help you, if they are negative they will hinder you. Sometimes you create happy thoughts and sometimes you create painful thoughts depending on your situation. Be assured that you can be anyone and do anything if you think so. WITH CONTINUOUS POSITIVE THOUGHTS, YOU CAN HAVE AS MUCH MONEY AS YOU CHOOSE. Program a thought in you than you will continually say and do things to bring that thought into objective reality. You will bring about your thought.

It is your continuous powerful thoughts that find ways to bring about the things you want and have in your life. If those thoughts are positive whatever you get in your life will make you feel positive. Your thoughts also work the opposite way. If your thoughts are, negative you will say and do negative things and you will see the results in your life. Use The Breath Method to program any thought you want in you. The application of Friendship with thought allows you to gain unbeatable advantages in any situation wherever you are. The implementation of Friendship with thought has transformation power to change you for the better. By applying Friendship with thought, you will think about and see people and things in a new light. You will see people as being part of you. You are not, frighten of you, likewise you would not be frighten of anyone when you think of them and see them as extension of you. You are continually sending out signals by what you say and do.

The signals you send out affect people either positive or negative by what they think and feel. If you focus, on the negative things of this world that is what you will see. When you think about the positive things of this world that is what you will see, feel and do. As a result, your world would be much happier. You will experience more of the wonderful things of this world. Find your place in this world. Do the things you really want to do. Be in the place you honestly want to be. Value the place and things that make you happy. This place of yours is something you have to discover for yourself. Only you will know when you have found it. However, you must be looking for that place of happiness. That place can be a literal place or it can be something you love doing. In order to find what you are looking for you need to have an inkling of what you are looking for.

You need to have some awareness of what will make you truly happy. In a state of awareness, you will notice your moments and what comes into your life. Noticing your moments will allow you to enjoy your life while being able to deal more adequately with any low moments. Thought is the key. Everyone and everything is a result of thought. You are thought experiencing life as a human. You are, thought experiencing yourself as a human. We all want to be happy, that is why we do the things we do. We all want to be in a state of prosperity. The information in these pages incorporates all you need to get you to a state of prosperity. When you are prosperous, you are happy. If you apply the information in these pages, you would be well on your way to prosperity and happiness. Happiness is largely a state of being which involves your mindset you will need to maintain that state of being including your mindset. You maintain your mindset by keeping your positivity alive. With your positivity alive, you can go ahead and do anything you want and achieve anything you want.

TONE

One grain of sand does not mean much, but put together they form a whole beach. One letter of the alphabet does not mean much but put together they can create very powerful words. Put together the right words and they become limitless. Words; has the ability to bring your spirit alive. By spirit I, mean your wonderful feelings. Words has verifying degrees of power to move us depending on the tone in which they are used. Especially so to our subconscious mind. Tone of words, have the power to create sensations, to alter thoughts and feelings according to the way they are used. Your tone of voice, reveal your true intentions. The same word can be said but in a different tone, and it will have a completely different meaning. The tone and meaning of words will affect you accordingly. A pleasant word when said harshly can have a negative meaning and effect on the listener. A not so pleasant word said in a mild gentle tone can have a positive response, it all depends on the tone in which it is said.

If you want people to take, notice of what you say use gentle, caring tones. The tone you use will come out in your speech and will be, picked up by your listeners. When someone make you feel happy by the things they say. You can keep those lovely thoughts and feelings to make you feel happy again by recalling them to mind. Whenever you use words, do your best to use tones that will uplift your listener. Most things we do we have learned. With practice, you can learn to master your tonality.

It's; what you have in you that matters. Your positive thoughts are very important. Without your positive thoughts, you would not do nor have anything of value. Without your positive, thoughts you would not be the person you are today. You do and have according to the thoughts you have in you. The strong thoughts and feelings you have in you are your beliefs. Your beliefs about you, makes you who you are. Your beliefs about you, makes you do the things you do. Your thoughts and feelings about certain people and things makes you believe certain things about them. When you believe, certain things about people or things you will act in accordance with those beliefs.

If you have, positive thoughts about them you will feel positive about them because you believe certain positive things about them. This belief is, built on evidence about those people and things. The evidence you have which you based your beliefs on about people and things can either be, true or false. As long as you accept that evidence those proof you will believe them. Your thoughts and feelings make you believe it, they make it so, they make it real. Keep in mind that your beliefs are, made up of thoughts and feelings. Your habitual regular, thoughts becomes your beliefs. Your beliefs become parts of you. Your beliefs are what make up the inner you, the inner self. You will act; you will behave according to your beliefs. The key to happiness is to stay in control of your thoughts. Positivity is the strongest energy in existence, which can be, manifested in thousands of different ways. Believe in things that brings you happy thoughts. What you believe in you get more of the same because our beliefs compel us to do according to what we believe.

You can live a life of ease, luxury and happiness while putting in minimum effort. You no longer have to work like a horse to have what you want to make you happy. That type of life is comparable to someone filling up a thousand-litre container of water ten miles from the source of the water using a ten litre-carrying container. Can you imagine the time and effort it will take to full that thousand litre container. However if that person had a truck with a thousand litre container that same job becomes much easier. Likewise, when you know the secrets of happiness and wealth it becomes much easier to do things to create happiness and wealth.

Thought will always be, thought will last forever and forever will never come. Thought is forever you are, thought manifested. The discovery that your true essence is, thought allows you to enjoy your life to the fullest. The purpose of thought is to maintain itself. Positive thoughts are the energy to overcome the resistance of negative thoughts. Positive thoughts build confidence. If you pretend, something long enough you will end up doing it. Even if you are, not as confident as you would like to be just pretend to be that you are confident. In time you, will be that which you are pretending to be because by pretending you are becoming that person. Believe you can and you will. A belief is a deep-seated thought, come what may you will act according to that belief. You need to like you to make you feel good. You need to make people feel good for them to like you.

The type of, life you live is largely dependent on whether you are an optimist or a pessimist. Optimism; has to be learned. If you leave, your state of being to chance without first developing an optimistic mentality it is very likely that you would gravitate toward pessimism. Build your optimism to the point where you would naturally see the beauty in all there is. It is your; wonderful optimistic energy that will get you whatever you want. When you are optimistic, your life will be happier, richer, and more purposeful. Your optimism will shine through in every area of your life. In time, all energy naturally fades. Besides there are so many things that can so easily drain your positivity energy. Your positive optimistic thoughts need fortifying regularly. Just as your body, need fortifying regularly for it to serve you well, so does your optimism. Keep in mind the pitch of your tone could determine how people respond to you. A low pleasant tone is calming and pleasant to listen too. A low pleasant tone makes its listeners feel secure. When people feel, secure they agree with you. When people agree with you, they will give you what you want. Remember to use low pleasant tones to get whatever you want.

CONFIDENCE

Believe that you can have as much money as you want and you will. Believe that you can have continuous positive thoughts as your predominant way of being and you will. Beliefs are the supports of all our actions. Beliefs are the support of our very being. Positive beliefs create positive actions. Negative beliefs create negative actions. If you have any negative thoughts about money or happiness, you will act accordingly towards happiness and money. Thus, you will need to change your thoughts about happiness and money. If you have the slightest belief that large sums of money is not for you; you need to change that belief. Use The Breath Method to install new thoughts and new feelings about money in you. Create the energy, the power of confidence to do what you want to do. Yes, confidence is, created either consciously or subconsciously. With the energy, of confidence you can do whatever you want.

Lack of confidence, is created mainly subconsciously when you tell yourself negative things about yourself. Negative thoughts about something you are about to do or something you are doing will diminish your confidence. Confidence is created by positive thoughts. Confidence is positive energy, the positive energy in you to do whatever you want to do. We experience that confidence, that power, that energy in the form of feelings. Have you ever heard the expression have confidence in yourself? Or. How big do you feel? Have you ever wondered what that really mean? Ask yourself. How much confidence; have you got inside of you to do and have the things you want? For example how much confidence have you got inside of you that you could have as much money as you want. When you are about to do something only think continuous positive thoughts about what you are about to do. With only pure, positive thoughts, you will have the confidence to do what you choose to do. Remember that it is your thought that creates your feelings.

If you are feeling nervous or scared, realize that it is you, who is creating those negative thoughts and feelings. You can just as easily create positive happy thoughts about your situation and you will experience your situation in a happy way. Friendship with thought is guaranteed to help you along your way to becoming wealthier, yes happier and richer. Friendship with thought can help you overcome your fears. For example, when you are walking down the road and you see someone coming towards you think of that person as, thought manifested, nothing more nothing less. You can use this same method for people or things. If you use, this method you will notice that it has an immediate effect. Your fears will immediately fade. Feeling confident, secure and happy comes from the conviction that you have the power to cope and overcome any tough time that comes your way. It is wise to bend gracefully in the face of strong winds than to stand ridged in the face of difficulties.

If you find, something difficult at present put it aside for a while then come back to it when you think the time is right. Belief and faith in yourself is essential to do and accomplish whatever you choose. Faith in you comes with practices. Your faith in you will get stronger with practice. Belief and faith in yourself will build your confidence. You can feel confident knowing that you are producing value for others, not everyone has this type of conviction and feelings. As you apply Friendship with thought in your life watch your awareness, confidence and good fortune unfold and flourish. The universe will start talking to you. You will see and hear conformation of your new prosperous life from people and things as if by coincidence as if by magic.

You will notice things that conform, the universe is being at your service, the universe is working on your behalf because you are in, sync with its purpose. For example, you will be walking or drive when a sign along the road will tell you exactly what you wanted to know. You will see or hear the answers you are looking for on TV or on a radio from programmes that it totally unrelated to the topic of the programme. You will be innocently minding your own business when someone say or do something, which was puzzling you before.

Yes, you will get clarifications from varied and unexpected sources. Welcome your sources and your changes. The meaning of life is to maintain thought. Strive to find your vocation, where you will say I am doing exactly what I want to do and I am enjoying it. As you continue along your journey, you will meet a stage where you could honestly say that you are doing what you want and it makes you happy. CHANGES ARE ALWAYS HAPPENING, BY IMPLEMENTING THIS INFORMATION YOU ARE GRADUALLY BRAKING FREE FROM YOUR PRESENT WAY OF LIFE. You are creating the confidence and courage to do anything you want. Do as much as you can to help others to be happy. Say as much as you can to help others to feel happy. You can have confidence and great joy knowing that you are being of service to others as well as to yourself. Find happiness in the knowledge that you are providing something of value to others.

OBJECTIVE REALITY AND IMAGINATION

We live in two worlds the world of objective reality and the world of our imagination our inner world. Be aware of your imagination and you will notice that your imagination never stops. From the day, you were born until now your imagination never stop. You have gotten used to your imagination to the point of not noticing it during your normal day's activities. Your power of imagination is very powerful and can work for you or against you. Your inner world, govern your outer world and are reflections of your inner world. If there are, conflicts between what you are imagining and what you are doing your imagination will win. For example you, may be going for something but telling yourself with your imagination that you do not deserve that which you are going for. You may want to do certain things but telling yourself with your imagination that you cannot do that which you would like to do. If you find, yourself in that type of situation you are sending out two conflicting signals and your imagination will win.

If you are going for something and you are imagining to yourself that you won't do it your imagination will compel you to act accordingly. You won't do what you want to do because you are imagining that you cannot do that. You are sabotaging yourself by sending out conflicting signals. You need to have your imagination working with you and for you if you are to succeed. You need to be in agreement with what you are doing and what you are imagining. If you are, going for something you really want you need to tell yourself with your imagination that you can do it or have it while going for it or doing it. If you tell yourself you can't do it or have it, you won't do it or have it. Imagine yourself, doing it or having it. In your imagination see, yourself doing whatever you want to do or having whatever you want to have and you will have it or do it. There are various names people use for this type of imagination. Some people call it visualization others call is creative thinking.

Some people say they cannot visualize when in fact they never stop visualizing. It is true that some people power of imagination is stronger than, others. However, we all have powers of imagination to varying degree. For example, do you know the colour of your shoe or the colour of the house you live in? Do you know the shape and colour of your front door, if you do than your power of imagination is working perfectly fine? Because we feel and behave as we imagine, have something or someone happy to fall back on during your days. Someone or something, that when you imagine them you will feel happy.

You are an automatic winner when you use Friendship with thought to make sense of the world. By applying Friendship with thought in your life, your imagination will automatically be positive. When your imagination, are predominantly positive, your experiences will be predominantly positive. Our experiences stay with us as memories, as thoughts of our past. Some of these past memories are pleasant and some are not so pleasant. Some are strong and vivid and some are faint, and need some focus thinking to recall them. Your happy memories are dependent on your happy thoughts and actions. The happy things you do today will be your happy memories tomorrow. Do as much happy things as you possible can and you will have an abundance of happy memories. Whatever your memories you do not have to be a prisoner or a slave to your memories you can change any unpleasant memory. To change any unpleasant memory, realize that it was only an experience. What you did to cause your experience you did it for the experience of it. Realize; that it is only your imagination of it that is keeping it alive.

Realize; that it is only what you are thinking about the experience that is making you happy or sad. You can view any experience in a more positive light if you choose to. By viewing your memories more positively they would feel less painful. Chances are if, other people did not tell you what you did was wrong you would not feel any guilt or pain from your experience. If other people were involved, they may have long been dead. Good or bad only the memory of them would remain. Remember that we are here for the experience of it. We are here to experience as much of human life as possible. Also, remember that we experience our own experiences. We create those experiences by the things we say and do. No one can experience our life for us but ourselves. I will remind you that Friendship with thought is a way of thinking and seeing everyone and everything as manifestations of thought.

Your thoughts give meaning to everything in your life. It is your thoughts you use to make sense of your experiences of life. You may have heard the expressions living in the present, living in the moment or living in the now. Your world of objective reality is what you experience in the now, in the present, in the moment with your five senses. Everything else is imagination, your imagination. That is not to say that your imagination is not real. Yes, your imagination is very real. Your world in your imagination is just as important as your world in objective reality. Some may argue that your world in your imagination is of greater importance since without your imagination your outside world would have no meaning to you. Your imagination is real but only to you. People will justify their imagination and behave accordingly. If need be you will find proof to justify any action based on your imagination.

As far as objective reality is concern, living in the moment of your five senses in objective reality is all there is. Everyone else and everything else outside of the moment is imagination. I am not saying that they may or may not exist what I am saying is as far as objective reality is concern in the now; they only exist in your imagination. What you can detect with your five senses is your world of objective reality as it stands in the present. Everything else is in your imagination. As stated above our world is made up of two planes from these two planes we get our experiences. What we can sense with our five senses we take as being real, exist in the material world. The world of imagination is just as real to the one doing the imagining. Have you ever had to give a presentation or had a job interview where your imagination took control to the point where you started to tremble.

Your hands may have started to shake, your lips went dry, or you may have even started to sweat. Your imagination could overwhelm you to the point where you feel physically sick thus the power of your imagination. Your imagination can work for you or against you. Imagine something good happening and you are letting your imagination work for you. If you imagine something going wrong or things not turning out as you want you are using your imagination against you. People quite often blur the lines of objective reality and imagination and create all sorts of problems for themselves. You need to, be aware that your imagination does create problems, especially things that do not exist in objective reality.

Be aware that you create pain of the past in the form of regrets or pain of fear of the future with your imagination. A common type of pain people create with their imagination is fear of doing. People love being safe and secure. They like the comfort and security of what they have come to know. People do not like changing that security and comfort that is part of their life. Even if that way of life is causing them pain, they will resist change. Doing for some people represent changes and they would rather stay as they are. The pay off for staying as they are is the security and comfort they feel with what is familiar to them. Even if what, is familiar to them is not what they want. People have important things they want to do or places they want to visit but stop themselves with their negative inner dialogue with their imagination. By using Friendship with thought in your life, you are applying a dual process of destroying negative imaginations and installing positive imaginations. When your imagination is predominantly positive about people and things, you will no longer be afraid of things that used to embarrass you or humiliate you. You would no longer be afraid of doing things to change. Instead, you will have the confidence, the power and energy to face and welcome any situation.

Your imagination can be your best friend or your enemy. Used properly your imagination can be your wonderful lifelong friend and helper. Use in the wrong way and your imagination can be like a prison of your own making keeping you exactly where you do not want to be. Be careful that you do not let negative imagination control your life. If you let, negative imagination control your life, your predominant experience of life will be negative. Your imagination has the power to make you happy or sad, to bring you pleasure or pain. Your imagination can make you rich or poor; it all depends on how you use it. When you use your imagination positively to imagine a happier way of life, a better way of life you will feel and see the good results as part of your life.

Be aware that you live in two worlds, your material world with your five senses in objective reality and your nonmaterial world, your world of your imagination. You spend a significant amount of time in your nonmaterial world. It is your nonmaterial world, your world of your imagination that determines your happiness and your predominant state of being. I'll remind you to be careful and be habitually aware of what you are imagining. Your imagination can run riot if you do not control it. You could easily, be sabotaging yourself without realizing that it is you who is stopping you from having and doing the things, you want. If you are not aware of what you are imagining you could be feeling down for too long.

Remember that you never stop thinking. Your imagination never stops. Regularly notice if what you are imagining is making you feel happy or sad. If what you are imagining is making you feel happy, good. If you are not feeling happy change what you are imagining. You create your own reality with your thoughts and your five senses. You give meaning to what you see, smell, taste, feel and hear. You interpret the outside world and make it your reality by what you think of it. Your imagination of your world becomes habitual to you. You get used to thinking and seeing your world as it is. If you create, your reality through predominantly negative thoughts your world will be dominated by negative people and things. Because that is how you interpret your world, your reality. Alternatively, if you create predominantly positive interpretations of your world your world will be full of happy positive people and things. The more positive happy people and things you have around you is the happier you will be. The more you associate, with people who are living the life you really want to live, is the more you will become one of them.

During your day, notice what you are imagining about people and things. If you catch yourself, imagining negative things change your thoughts. We are always imagining something but we are not always aware of what we are imagining. Your imagination can be a friend or an enemy. If your imagination is an enemy it will work against you without you quite knowing what's going wrong. You will be trying your best but the enemy within you will be sabotaging you, your imagination will be working against you if you let it. If you are not habitually aware of what you are imagining you could be sabotaging your efforts. On the other, hand when your imagination is a friend of yours your life is much happier. Things fall into place easily and habitually. This is because you have imagined things going well for you without quite being aware that you are imagining those things. And you act according to those positive thoughts to bring about your positive results.

Keep in mind that you may want to be predominantly happy but if your imagination is predominantly negative, there is no way you will be predominantly happy. If you catch, yourself creating the future you do not want through your negative imagination change what you are imagining. Your habitual imagination creates your habitual state of being. You can create your life as you imagine it to be.

GESTURES

According to social scientist, humans use two types of language, nonverbal and verbal as a reflection of their thoughts. Nonverbal communication or gestures with our body, hands and arms show our thoughts. Gestures help add meaning to what we are saying they make visible our thoughts. Gestures are types of visible communications they reveal our true thoughts. Our, body movements are connected to our thinking and speaking. While speaking the things we do with our body are saying something about how we feel. People could be talking to you but saying something different with their body. We communicate our attitude our personality by use of our nonverbal language. The verbal use of language is to communicate knowledge in a more detailed manner. Body language is most effective in communicating our feelings. Body language signals our wants and desires in a most subtle and powerful manner. For example when people are romantically attracted to each other, they will use body language in a number of ways to signal this to each other. We use verbal language primarily to communicate about the world. Nonverbal communication is use mainly for human relationships. Your nonverbal signals; are connected to your emotions about how you feel about certain people and things.

We attract what we habitually think and feel with our nonverbal communication. What nonverbal signals are you sending out? How are you feeling about certain people and things? We send out nonverbal signals of people and things by what we think and feel about certain people and things. These signals are reflected by our body our heads our faces and especially our hands. Next time you are in a conversation notice what you and the person you are talking to are doing with your hands and heads. Usually all of, these movements are done subconsciously. We are all constantly sending out signals. Yes, everyone and everything are sending out signals just for the fact of being. We sometimes consciously and deliberately send out certain signals. However, the majority of the signals we send out we do so subconsciously.

You may want someone or something as part of your life but if you are not sending out the right signals no matter how hard you try you will not get what you want. To get what you want you must send out the right signals.

Habitually be aware of the signals you are sending out. You must think and feel good, happy, pleased and accepting of the people and things you want as parts of your life. When they pick, up these positive signals they will be attracted to you. Like it or not we all gesture as we speak without quite being aware that we are gesturing. You can think of gestures as expressions of your thoughts, representations of your thoughts. You let people see what you are thinking with your gestures. Gesturers are used, mainly subconsciously as we speak that is why they reveal our hidden thoughts as we speak. To get what you want make sure that your gestures, the signals you are sending out, are saying the same thing as you are speaking. Yes, you can tell people how you feel about them without words. Our faces reveal our thoughts and feelings without words. Our bodies and faces movements reveal our thoughts and feelings. Whatever you say and do, do it with a pure positive motive. Your pure motive will be reveal by your body movements, including your tone of voice. Your pure motivation should also be present when you do your action.

CHANGE

To get all those wonderful things you want in your life you must be willing to change. If you continue, the same way you will continue to get the same people and things. To do and have all those wonderful things you want as part of your life you not only need to be willing to change you must change. You must change to the type of person who do and have those wonderful things you want. You need to have the type of personality and attitude of those people who have the type of things you want. You can be whoever or whatever you want to be. You need to learn new habits; your new positive habits will automatically replace your old limiting habits. The road to change is to pick your ideal positive qualities then become familiar and comfortable with them. Make them your new habits. Use The Breath Method to install in you your new qualities.

Keep on practicing your new qualities, your practice will reinforce these qualities. I know the word practice to some means boring hard work. As you will find out The Breath Method is as easy and natural as breathing itself. As long as you are able to breathe, practice would not be a problem for you. As you continue, to use The Breath Method you will get use to it. Your new attitude and personality will soon become a natural part of you. You must, truly and honestly want to grow. Growth involves changes. You must honestly want to change it's the only way to grow. There are many factors and many ways to create growth and happiness. It is often, said that the paths to happiness is as numerous as the stars in the sky. No one single nation holds a monopoly on happiness, awareness and enlightenment.

To find your way follow the path that is more attune to your personality, the path that you are more happy and comfortable with. You will always exist in one form or another that is what makes it O.K. When you know everything will be OK, no matter what you have no worries. When you do not worry, you are more secure and free to experience your life to your full potential. Learn to stop worrying. If you continue, to worry your worries will stop you from enjoying your life to the full. The thought of knowing that it is O.K. creates happiness in people. Having Friendship with thought as part of your personality, as part of your attitude and as part of your life will generate happy feelings in you. By using Friendship, with thought there are no confrontations with anyone, not only for our own thoughts and well-being but also for that of others. People are, naturally frighten of changes. However, changes will always happen; you can learn to make change happen in ways that will help you. For you to do have and be what you choose, changes must take place. If you do not help change, you will get more of the same. Accept changes as important, important and vital to what you want to have. Without changes, you will never get to where you want to be.

By accepting that people and things will change, that there will always be changes you automatically remove any fear to do things that will change your experience of life. You must accept that change is inevitable; it's the nature of the universe. Any good moral cause is worth the effort you put into it. You can feel confident and happy that you have and are using the resources to make many people's lives happier and better. You can choose to create and take your freedom, your liberation from negative cycles of lack, to a state of predominant happiness where lack has cease to exist. It is fear in various forms that is keeping you from having and doing what you want. To have what you want easily you need to overcome your fears of that which you want. To create a continuous state of abundance you need to overcome your fear of lack and poverty. Remember that we will do according to what we think and feel. To overcome any fears have something wonderful to put in its place. For example, if you are fearful of having an, interview it is what you are thinking about the interview that is making you feel fearful. Think instead of going on a wonderful holiday or anything else that will take your attention away from fear. Think about someone or something that make you feel happy. When you are happy, you are not afraid. The more you think about someone or something; is the more you will feel according to how they make you feel when you think about them. Yes, we can all definitely do things to change.

BELIEFS

All negative thoughts can be broken. By taking in positivity, by developing positivity there will come a day when the good in you begin to flow. There will come a day when your happiness begins to flow more freely. With your positivity flowing, any negativity you had is fast fading. You can create and develop any belief you want. Belief is the energy to do. Belief has great power. Beliefs work. With belief, there is no doubt. With belief, there is no question of doubt. Belief is free of doubt. Our planet is the way it is because of people beliefs. The buildings, roads and everything else are manifestations of our beliefs. Your positive beliefs will get you there, to wherever you want to be. Have you ever heard the expression that you must believe in yourself? To believe in yourself is to, honestly think something positive about you and to, habitually think those thoughts. For example to believe in your self is to honestly think that you are able or capable to do or have something if you really want to.

Believing in yourself also includes honestly thinking that you are worthy and deserving of the good things in life. Yes, you have to think it to believe it. Without positive self-beliefs in you, mainly negative self-beliefs would remain in you. If predominantly negative beliefs remain in you, you will sabotage yourself without quite being aware that you are sabotaging your efforts. You need to make sure that you have in you, mainly positive beliefs about you. Remember to succeed you need to think and feel positive and confident about yourself in relation to what you want. Here are four powerful positive beliefs to help you along your way. Honestly believe you, are worth it. Honestly, believe it can happen. Honestly believe you, can succeed. Honestly believe you, deserve it. Use Friendship with thought to help you develop your honest positive beliefs. You can just as easily learn to think positively just as easy as you have learned to think negative. You need to take a conscious deliberate part in your thinking to make them positive.

If you live, them to chance chances are they are likely to be negative depending on how much negative thoughts you have in you. Our thoughts are food for the mind. Yes, our thoughts are energy for the mind. Society send out, predominantly negative thoughts. Society feed people predominantly negative food for their minds. If you recognize that you are dining on mainly negative thoughts that society is dishing out you need to stop eating at society table. I know it is not easy to buck the trend. It is much easier to go with the crowd. It can even be a little bit frightening to be an independent thinker. However, independent thinkers are in control of what they choose to believe. Independent thinkers are leaders and trendsetters they lead while others follow. That is the natural nature of independent thinkers. Your beliefs will give you the life you believe is yours. Wanted or unwanted you will live the life you believe you deserve.

Right or wrong, you will live the life you believe you are worth. We are compelled to live in accordance with our beliefs. Very often, we cannot see anything wrong with our beliefs or our way of life. If you have beliefs that are more positive in you, you are more likely to believe you can do anything you want. If you have predominantly negative thoughts in you, your self-esteem will be low. With low self-esteem you will habitually be putting yourself down, you will habitually put yourself last. Because you do, not believe you deserve to take first place. With high self-esteem, the sky is your limit.

Some beliefs are stronger than, others. We all have certain beliefs. When you believe you can do it that belief will support you to do it. Your beliefs make you special. You are who you are because of your beliefs. You do the things you do because of your beliefs. We are all different we have similar experiences of life but different. You can never, not believe something. People will do according to their beliefs. You can never, not do, something. We must believe something. Believing is a, need it's the way we are made. Just as we, are made with the need for air, and food similarly we are made with the need for beliefs. Could you imagine if you had to remember every single detail about life without beliefs? Without beliefs, you simply would not function. Right or wrong if people believe certain things they will act in accordance with their beliefs. Beliefs are what support our actions. Right or wrong from our point of view, people will live their life according to their beliefs.

People in general inherit their beliefs. They do not question those beliefs they think that their beliefs are the ideal way. Those beliefs could be doing more harm than good if they are not getting you the people and things you want to be part of your life. Remember for a belief to be a belief there is no question about that belief. A belief is basically, a deep-seated thought. Ask questions about your beliefs if you are not satisfy with the life you are living. Question your beliefs; about certain things that you are unhappy about. Look for different answers to familiar routines. There are always different ways of doing the same things with better results. If you continue to believe the same things, you will continue to do the same things and get the same results. If you want a better result, you need to do things differently. You need to believe that things can be, done differently with better results. Our beliefs are the essence of our being. Our beliefs support who we think we are. Your beliefs give you your identity. Your beliefs tell you know who you are and you will act accordingly. It is because of our beliefs we do whatever we do. Our survival depends on our beliefs. You will prosper or you will live in lack because of the things you believe.

Let your beliefs work for you instead of against you. You let your beliefs work for you by believing that you deserve certain good things. You let your beliefs work for you by creating a new personality and developing the attitudes you really love. When you continually think the way that new person you have created think you will come to believe in your new personality. Let your beliefs work for you by believing that you deserve to be happy. Believe the things, you want are possible, it is very likely that most of what you want already exist. Believe me that it is only negative thoughts about what you want that is preventing you from having them. Replace any negative thoughts about whatever you want with pure positive thoughts and you are likely to do and have what you want. If you truly, believe that you deserve the best you will act accordingly. You will do things to have the best. Believe you can do those wonderful things that you always wanted to do if you really want to and you will do them. Remember when we believe certain things we will act in accordance with those beliefs. Our beliefs will compel us to behave according to what we believe.

Your self-belief is the amount to which you believe deep inside of you that you are worthy and deserving of the good things of this world. The things that will make you feel happy. If you truly believe this, you will automatically feel it and you will act accordingly. Even if at, the moment you do not think and feel that, you are worthy and deserving to be happy, to enjoy the good things of this world you can develop that belief. Without positive self-belief, you will habitually sabotage yourself without quite knowing why, certain things always seems to go wrong. If you do, not believe you are worth it and deserve it you will not keep it even if someone gave it to you. With low, self esteem if you, are consciously going for something you want you will be telling yourself otherwise subconsciously.

You will be telling yourself with your imagination that you do not worth it. If you tell, yourself you do not deserve it or do not worth it you will act in certain ways to sabotage yourself from having it. You must convince yourself that you are worthy and deserving of anything that will make you happy. In short, you must believe you are worthy and deserving of whatever you want and choose. With these types, of positive belief in you, you will automatically act accordingly to bring about the things you have chosen. Use The Breath Method to help you install whatever beliefs you want in you. Use The Breath Method to convince yourself that you deserve, good health, that large sum of money, that house, or anything else you want. Believe that you are worthy and deserving of anything that will bring you happiness. You need to convince yourself that you are worthy of the good things of life. Keep in mind it is what you think about those things, which will make you happy. You can have the best but think little of it and it won't bring you happiness. Your ideal life is what you think it is. Choose the life you want, you can make your dreams come true. You can only do it if you think and believe you can. Use the Breath Method to build up your self-belief.

For example, when using the word worthy with your mouth firmly close and slowly inhaling only through your nose. Repeat slowly to yourself **I am worthy of the good things of this world.** As you, exhale slowly only through your nose. Repeat slowly to yourself **I am worthy of the good things of this world**. The idea is to say the whole sentence in one slow breath. For example, when using the word deserve, with your mouth firmly close and inhaling only through your nose. Repeat slowly to yourself **I deserve to have and enjoy the good things of this world.**

Repeat the same sentence as you exhale slowly only through your nose. If you have a block nose, you can still do this installation. You must breathe only through your mouth by holding your nose and say your sentence in your mind. You will immediately feel the effects of what you are saying to yourself.

You can use The Breath Method to install any positive word or phrase about yourself in you.

By using The Breath Method in conjunction with Friendship with thought, you will create an unbreakable bond of friendship with who-ever or whatever you want. As you use it you will immediately feel it, that feeling is how you know that it is in you. Keep on doing it until it becomes a powerful part of you. Keep in mind that Friendship with thought is your new positive way of thinking and seeing people and things. You see people and things as thought manifested in various forms. You can love or like whoever or whatever you choose. You only need; your permission to create your strong friendship with who-ever or whatever you choose. You give yourself your permission by liking or loving whoever or whatever you choose.

You need the help of discipline in order to continue to do what you choose to do in order to achieve the things you want. You need strong determination to help you along your way to have what you think will make you happy. Because our thoughts change and our feelings fade, you will not feel exactly, the same every day. Sometimes you will feel that you can take on the world and sometimes you will feel less enthusiastic. However, with these natural laws and principles in operation in your life you will be more positive. You will feel more enthusiastic with them than without them, this I promise you. When you are not feeling on top of the world, you will need the help of discipline to carry you along, to keep you moving forward to your dreams. Once you have installed more positive energy in you than are negative energies these positive energies will keep you going. However, you will need to keep on tapping up your positive energy. By establishing a routine, a habit of doing certain things your routine will keep you going in any rough weather. With your positive habits, and your routine in place you will continue on your course.

Change; usually involve a certain amount of discomfort that is why you will also need the help of discipline, positive habits and routine. Because of the, law of duality there will be times when you don't feel like doing what you know you must do. The law of duality states that there must always be an opposite. With this information, you can expect some days to be more exciting than, others. You may have a setback on certain projects of yours. These setbacks are what I call the rough weather. When sailors on board ships come across rough weather, they button down the hatches and ride out the bad weather. The ship continues on its course to its destination. Your goals are your destination. You may come across rough weather on your journey towards your destination. If you come across rough weather just keep in mind that there will be rough weather and there will be good weather. There is always calm after the stormy weather. It is then your-self discipline routine and positive habits will be on your side. They will be your allies to help you towards your destination.

With determination, you will ride out the rough weather and arrive at your destination. You will finish what you have started. Using Friendship with thought, your journey will be much easier than without Friendship with thought. Keep in mind that everything we do has to do with our thoughts. It all depends, on how we view people and things; that includes our situations and the experiences we had from those situations. By thinking and viewing your situations in a more positive light, you will be better place to deal with them more successfully.

Be extra careful of what comes into your mind. Be aware of your habitual imagination because you will behave according to what comes into your mind. Yes, you will act according to your imagination. Your imagination is, like a two edge sword, it can protect you or it can harm you. If you think positively the sword will protect you. If you think, negatively the sword will harm you. Believe what you want can be owned by you and you will own it if you want. If you believe you can swim not being able to swim does not come into your mind. You will just do it; you will just swim without thinking about it. If you believe you can ride a bicycle not being able to ride a bicycle does not cross your mind. Keep in mind that your beliefs are your supports for your actions. You will do, as you believe. If you want to do a certain thing and you believe you can do it, you will go ahead and just do it without questioning whether you can do it or not. It is your beliefs that provide the energy for your actions. You will need the help and support of your beliefs to get the wonderful things you want out of life.

Our beliefs can support us, providing us with the will to do. Alternatively, our beliefs can work against us by filling us with fear. It is only your fear that is stopping you from having the life you want to live. If you were, not frighten of doing certain things you would go right ahead and do them. It is by doing things that people succeed. When you get rid of your fears of doing you will do whatever is necessary to have whatever you want without causing any harm. Positive or negative, if you believe it you will do it accordingly. When our beliefs are working for us on our side there is no force in the universe that can stop us from achieving our aims. Keep in mind that we create our own beliefs.

We create our own energy our own will to do whatever we want to do. You are using the same energy, the same creative force that has been use to create everything in existence. You use the same creative energy to do everything you do. Yes, you use that same energy that same creative force every time you do something. You are the source of that energy; you are the source of that power. You generate that energy, that power with your positive thought. When you want, something or you want to do something. All you have to do is create that positive thought which will create that energy to do, that power to do and you will do whatever you choose to do you will have create the will to do.

Here is how you do it.

EVERY DAY "THINK" ABOUT THE THINGS YOU WANT TO DO OR THE THINGS YOU WANT TO HAVE AND YOU WILL DO THINGS TO DO OR HAVE WHAT YOU WANT. You will be creating the energy to do, the power to do, the will to do in order to do to have or do what you want.

Realize that doing can also include just sitting there. Someone may ask what is, he doing. The reply may come back he is just sitting there. What is he doing, he is sitting there. Although he is, just sitting there he is still doing something. He is sitting. We can never, not do, something. Is what you are doing helping or hindering you? Is what you are doing helping you to get what you want? Whatever you are, doing it is because of your beliefs. Are your beliefs helping you to achieve what you want? Whatever you have, in your life it is because of your beliefs. Whatever you make of your life it is because of your beliefs. Your beliefs can either, push you forward with happiness or they can hold you back with sadness. The life you live it is because of what you believe. Yes, your way of life is because of the things you believe. Our beliefs are our guide through life. Where is your guide taking you? Are you happy where your guide is taking you? Beliefs can and does change. Certain things you used to believe when you were a child you may no longer believe. New evidence may have come along to persuade you otherwise.

For example, you may have believed that education was only for the rich. In certain countries, education was and in some areas still is, believed to be the sole domain of men. These beliefs are slowly changing. Yes, beliefs can change. If your beliefs are not serving you, you can change them. The easiest way to change any belief is to create or find evidence to support your new belief. You now know that education is open to all so you no longer believe that education is the sole domain of men. If you are not happy where your beliefs are taking you, you can change them. Your world is a manifestation of your beliefs. People do or do not do things because of what they believe.

Belief is not the sole domain of men or of religion. People do all sorts of things and justify them in the name of God, with their religion. What may believe to be wrong in one country may be perfectly O.K. in another country. The world as it is are; results of our beliefs not only religious beliefs but beliefs in general. According to your, beliefs you would not do or do certain things. What you think about and what you believe about yourself determines what you say do and feel about you in relation to others. The world around, you reflect your inner world, your thoughts, your beliefs. For example if you believe you are becoming more positive, your external world will confirm this belief. You will notice, and compare situations and things while feeling upbeat to confirm your belief. While at the same time deflecting or ignoring anyone or anything which; does not match your beliefs.

Any limiting belief you may have in you will cost you something. Negative beliefs stop people from saying and doing what they really want to say or do. For example, you may hear of a well paying job with excellent prospects. If you believe that, you are not good enough for that job, even if that job were, given to you. You will say and do things to let the job slip away from you and put it down to bad luck.

YOUR WONDERFUL SITUATIONS

I would like to share a story with you about a group of people who were, given opportunities to better themselves materially. The first group is about a family who was, given a wonderful brand new family house in a nice neighbourhood. About six months later, I could not believe my eyes. Although one could tell that, the house was new, it was in a terrible state. The mentality of, those people who were given that brand new house just did not fit that house and neighbourhood. In a very short while the house was almost ruin. The second example involves a man who came into a large sum of money. This man was about in his late sixties early seventies. The money he came into was more than enough to see him comfortable for the rest of his life. In a relatively, short while he was back in his original position.

The reason for these two experiences is to demonstrate that out habitual thoughts creates our situations and experiences of life. The first experience with the family and the new house in that nice neighbourhood demonstrates that this was no place for them unless they change their habitual thoughts. Unless people change, their dominant thoughts they will continue to do the same things. Their thoughts become apparent by the life they live. Thus, they continue to do and get the same results, which will keep them exactly where they are. The second experience of the man who came into a large sum of money also demonstrates. For people to accept their new situations they must be willing to embrace new experiences a new way of life. Without change of, thoughts with regard to our attitude and personality in relation to a different way of life there is only one option, more of the same. Our thoughts and actions create our situations and our situations create our experiences.

To experience life differently we must create something differently, our thoughts. Use Friendship with thought and the Breath Method to help you create and install new thought patterns. Situations are very important. It is situations; we use to create our life as we experience it. As we experience our situations, so we experience our lives. Positive situations are what produce wealth and happiness. Negativity only destroy, however there has to be a balance and negativity provide this balance. You do not have to be a negative person. Consciously or unwittingly, there are plenty of people, who will provide that type of energy. How would you feel if you could create and use any situation to your advantage? Positive qualities will create similar situation to themselves. Thoughts and actions of confidence, love, awareness, joy, and happiness will create similar situations. Negative qualities will produce negative situations. Negative situation is what produces poverty and pain. Anger, habitual complaining, greed, fear and laziness will create similar negative situations. We create all situations we are in either consciously or subconsciously. You can easily consciously, create the situation you want and choose to be in. Just as you create situations subconsciously, you can just as easily create situations consciously as you choose. We create our situations by what we think about and do. Positive thoughts and actions create positive situations. Negative thoughts and actions create negative situations. We derive our experiences from our situations.

You can take control of your situations now and in the future just by what you think about it. Negative thoughts cause pain, fear, and all sorts of unwanted feelings. Fear stops people from realizing their true potential. By being free from negative thoughts about yourself, people or things you will be free to create your life according to your choice. You can create a life of peace, prosperity, happiness and abundant wealth. Whether you are happy, enjoying it or having fun or not in your current situation, you created it. The fact that you are in a situation means that you have contributed to the creation of that situation. Situations give us all we have and do. Yes, your situation delivers everything you have or do to you. The people and things in your life positive or negative you extracted them or it from your situation to create your next situation.

Your habitual thoughts creates, makes your situations. Every situation you are in belongs to you. You have put yourself in it by what you have thought, said and done. If you take a few moments to think about it, you will realize this to be true. Take your friends for example, had you not went where you did you would not have met those individuals on that particular occasion. Some people call, this fate nevertheless, we create our own fate. Yes, we create our situations and our state of being with our thoughts. You can control your situation with pure positive thought of love. By love, I mean that you are not thinking anything negative about anything or anyone including yourself. If you want, something or you want to do something stick to that wonderful thought of doing or having that which you want. By sticking to your thought, you will bring it about into objective reality.

When you are not fearful, you are confident and when you are confident, you are in control of you. You like me want to be happy. When you honestly say wonderful things and do wonderful things to make people happy they will willingly drop their guard and give over control to you. Thus, you can take over control of the situation, all because you honestly making people feel positive and happy. Keep in mind that people all over the world want to be happy. That is their number one concern. We extract everything we have and do from our situations. Make your predominant thoughts pure positive thoughts and you will create predominantly pure positive situations for yourself and others. Only the individual can put sufficient positive energy to become competent, happy and prosperous. Because they alone have knowledge of them-self and what is best for them of what is enough for them. All we have are reflections of our thoughts in any given situation. Keep in mind that the situation you are in gives you your experiences of life.

Friendship with thought people can easily rid themselves of negative thoughts and all negative situations. They can create almost immediately the situation they want. By freeing yourself from all negative thoughts your pure positive thoughts will lead you to people and things that will trigger happiness in you. You will automatically say and do positive things. Yes by being free from negative thoughts your positive thoughts will be more powerful to create the happiness you desire. Remember that happiness, is made up of positive thoughts and action that brings about a state of well-being the feelings we call happiness.

Keep in mind that positive or negative, you created it and will experience it accordingly. If you decide to take control of your situations, you will be happier when you consciously create situations that make you happy. Anyone can live the life they have ever dreamed of by habitually creating pure positive thoughts, which will create feelings and situations accordingly. You create the situation with the people and things you want to experience. Then you need to do something to extract from that situation who or what you want from it. The ideal situation is when you are producing value for others.

The production of values, create high-self esteem. High self- esteem produces happiness. People self-esteem is an estimation of what they think they are good enough or not good enough to do or have. Self-esteem is largely dependent on one's effectiveness in dealing with any situation he or she may be in. A high level of self-esteem requires a commitment to pure positive thoughts. One must always put forth effort to create and importantly maintain positive thoughts or they will fade and die. Remember that your self-esteem is your thoughts and feelings about yourself. Of being, worthy and deserving to continuously live in prosperous, peaceful, happy situations. Sense of self will determine what you do and choose in life. You retain and maintain your happy sense of self by continually and consciously, rejecting all negative thoughts of self and others.

People have the right to create and live for their happiness. Your happiness is link to your self-esteem. The development of your self-esteem is important to feel worthy of any situation, person or thing that gives pleasure, peace, prosperity, love, wealth and happiness. The beliefs you hold will shape your life for better or for worse, for happy or for sad. If you believe, if you think and feel that you are not worthy of it no matter how hard you try you just won't do it or have it because you think it's too good for you. That is because we are compelled to behave, to act, to do in accordance with our beliefs. This is why it's so very important to have positive high self worth. This is why it's so important to develop your high self worth, your wonderful self-esteem. How long it, takes you to honestly believe that you can do something is the time it will take for you to do it. By honestly I mean with no doubt included. No buts' no ifs. Just pure positive, thoughts about what you want or what you want to do.

I'll remind you, to get what you want out of life you need to have the energy to do what is necessary to have what you want. You need to have faith in you and your abilities that you can do what it takes to get you there. We do not always see ourselves as other people see us. I will have at a guest that some people have faith in you and your abilities to do certain things that you think you cannot do. If others put faith in your abilities, it is an indication that you have some hidden talents that you do not recognize in yourself. If others put their trust in you, so can you also put trust in yourself?

If you find yourself in that enviable situation, develop the attitude that you will give the best of your abilities. When you do, you will be using something not everyone has. You will be using what you have for your happiness and the happiness of others. As you, start succeeding, you will conclude that you can do, have and be whatever you want. You will be convinced that you have the ability because you are using it and are getting good results. If others can see certain ability in you do not deny that ability, use it for your advantage and the benefit of others.

Yes if others can see that, you have the ability and potential for greatness use those gifts of yours. We all have; certain abilities and potential that are valuable as gold and diamonds. They are usually, buried deep within us. If yours are, at the surface use them. Usually it's the things people find so easy that they can do them easily with their eyes close.

While most people, would be struggling to do the very same thing. It's very easy for some gifted people to take their gifts for granted that they do not even consider their gift because it is so easy for them. The fact that others see them in you means that they are at the surface. Use them for your and others benefit. If you continue, denying your abilities you could easily be sabotaging yourself; with yourself doubt. If you find, you have an ability to do something easily very likely people are waiting to pay good money for that thing. There is an old English saying that there is a buyer for everything. You may be easily wasting something of value to others and yourself. There is an old Jewish saying that says look after others and others will look after you.

If you have certain talent that is apparent to others and you continue to believe that you do not have it you are limiting yourself. Those limiting beliefs are not apparent to you yet. If you deny that, you can do certain things you are denying yourself of happiness. You are undermining your own self if you deny your, potential and abilities. If you find this to be true of you, you may be letting doubts and fears hold you back. By the time you finish reading this book you will know exactly how to dissolve those doubts and fears.

Happiness, love, prosperity and well-being involve the whole person. Happiness involves your thoughts, feelings, and body. To regularly, be happy just link happiness with every person and things in all your situations and you will be predominantly happy. You already do this mainly subconsciously on a daily basis. Now you are going to do it consciously and deliberately. When you think of your pay cheque at the end of the month how do you feel? When you think of your favourite food, how do you feel? When you think of someone or something, you like or love, how do you feel? Yes, you feel happy, that is because you have linked happiness to them. Usually this linking, of happiness to people and things is done subconsciously. You cannot be anything but mainly happy in all situations if you link every person and things in your life with happiness. I know this will take effort; this is the price, you must be willing to pay. As you first start linking people and things to happiness you may be tested to thinking, this is too hard. The more you do this linking people and things in your life to happiness is the easier it will become. You will reach a stage where it becomes almost effortless to link happiness to people situations and things.

You can use Friendship with thought knowledge to gain power and wealth in any situation. Just by making the knowledge of Friendship with thought, your own as part of your life you will automatically know how to take control. You can take control of any situation to give yourself happiness quickly, easily and almost effortlessly. Some people may say that this is selfish, that you are exploiting people. Let me say to you, first of all that it is not exploitation and secondly this is naturally continually happening every single day of your life. You are always in a situation. It is a natural way of life, which you have been engaged in all your life. Only now, you are in the driving seat, in control. No one can be in control of your situation for you; it is a sole individual responsibility of life.

This knowledge when applied can stop the pain or harm trigger by some everyday acquaintances. You will know how to deal with the situation. We are always in a particular situation. We are constantly moving from one situation to the next. Our situation gives us our experiences of life. By developing your creative qualities such as positive thoughts, happy feelings, confident doing and feeling calm and relax with time. All such qualities become limitless powerful tools at your disposal to create the life you choose. Those tools are what make it possible for you to do the work of making your dreams become realities.

Using Friendship with thought, thoughts, you can break free from all negative thoughts and live a guiltless fearless life of power, wealth, pleasure, and luxury. Whatever you choose to achieve give it some deep positive happy thoughts. Because this is the energy, you are creating and attaching to the object of your desire. This is the energy you will have from the object of your attention once you have created it in your life. Your ability to see people and things as wonderful thoughts manifested is always with you in any situation. Find the happy positive thought in any situation you are in and you take control of that situation. When you do, you become a winner. By taking control, I mean taking control of you. Taking control of your thought, thinking only positive pure thoughts about yourself and everyone involved. Habitually see people and things as thoughts manifested the same as you. Make that your new predominant way of thinking and seeing the world. When you do, you will soon feel confident enough to take the lead in any situation. Look and you will find that situations are what hold the potential to produce everything in your life.

If you do not like a certain situation, you can change it. You start by looking and seeing happy ways you can change your situation. Even if that way is only small, it does matter because change has a knock on effect. Make, absolutely sure that, that little change feels happy because however it feels is the same feelings it will create in your new situation. Remember that you are the one that creates all your situations even if you are not consciously aware of that fact. Yes, consciously or subconsciously we create our own situations. You will feel your power of confidence grow as you learn to use your knowledge of Friendship with thought. I will remind you that Friendship with thought is a new way of thinking, seeing and experiencing people and things as all thoughts manifested. Remember we must first think it, before we can make it or have it. The things you have if you did not think about them then someone else did. You may not know who made them but someone did. We live in an intelligent universe, we can see design everywhere we look.

By using happy thoughts, feelings, doing and time, you will be more excited about whatever you have to do. This excitement will make you want to get on with it. By, deciding to be a productive person, by using Friendship with thought. You; will be protected from all harmful situations. This protection will come about because of your positive thoughts. It's impossible to be cross with a cheerful, happy, confident person. Your cheerful, happy, confident disposition will create cheerful, happy, and peaceful situations. Once you have rid yourself, of negative thoughts about what you have to do you will automatically and naturally flourish because you will do whatever you choose. You will prosper easily. Once you free yourself of habitual negative fearful or lazy thoughts you become powerful to do, to accomplish any and everything your heart desire. You will easily create and take control of any situation you choose.

Lasting happiness, prosperity and well-being comes from continuous development of our personality and attitude. Yes, from the development of our pure positive thoughts towards people and things. At the same, time producing competitive values in the form of goods or services for others. When you fully understand and accept thoughts as the creator of all there is. You will become aware that your life is the way you see it because of your interpretations of it. It is because of your thoughts you experience life the way you do. When you habitually think, that life is good that people are good that you are good you are making it that way. Continue to think that you are valuable and are worthy of a happy life. Feel that you are worthy to live a wonderful luxurious life of happiness and prosperity. When you make this way of thinking and feeling your way of thinking and feeling, you will make it your way of life. You will become that person that, live such a wonderful life.

When you naturally think this way, you will know for sure that you are growing, that you are going in the right direction. Keep in mind that we create our experiences from our situations. Negative thoughts produces negative situations and diminishes every value it is expose to including humans. We live in a world that appears to profit from negativities. Negativity does not produce happiness. To become prosperous, successful and happy dismiss all negative thoughts made either by your-self or by others. When you create and have within you pure positive thoughts about you or your situation. You will have powerful control over all your situations. Positive thoughts create and are conducive to happy positive situations and values in everyone and everything it touches.

Success means different things to different people. What does success mean to you? For some success is the attainment of power or wealth, for others success is the realisation of their goals. Success can be, likened to a wonderful cake. Have you got; all the ingredients for success? To bake your wonderful cake of success you will first have to decide what type of cake you will bake. Then you will have to gather the ingredient. Next, you will have to follow the recipe for your wonderful cake.

If you follow the recipe carefully, the result will be your wonderful cake. Yes, you will have a wonderful cake to enjoy. I think you like me will share your wonderful cake with your family and friends. It is the same with success if you follow the recipe of success you will succeed in all you do. THE RECIPE OF SUCCESS INCLUDES YOUR AIM, POSITIVITY, CONFIDENCE, AND DOING. For example, if you want large sums of money you will have to sell things at a profit. Select something as your aim, something that you like. It does not matter what as long as it is legal and you like it. When you are selling something that is legal, there is no need to look over your shoulder. Your mind will be free to focus on your success. Whatever you select should have the potential to sell millions. What you choose should make you feel happy. You need to think and feel positive about what you have chosen.

You will need to be confident by thinking and feeling confident about the success of your goal. Finally, you will have to "do"; you will have to take action to make your dream a reality. With your aim, positivity, confidence and doing in your control you are half way there. I'll repeat what I have just said. With your aim, positivity, confidence and doing in your control you are half way there. Yes half way to achieving your aim. All you have to do now it to remember to continue to be positive about your aim as you do to achieve your aim. Think only continuous positive thoughts about your aim. Be confident about your aim. When you think about your aim, it should make you happy. Habitually think only positive confident thoughts about your aim. Follow the first and second steps for having your aim and the third step will be easy. Once you have built your positive attitude and confidence towards your aim, you will find it a joy to do things making your aim, your dream a reality, your reality.

Only you know your true aims. You choose your aim, your goal. Use Friendship with thought to dissolve your fears by how you think about people and things this includes things you will have to do to have your aim. Be positive about, people and things you will encounter as you go about doing things to achieving your aims. Use The Breath Method to install, to program your thoughts with what you have to do to achieve your goals. Negative feelings can stop you from doing things to achieve your aims. Even in the, family you can sometimes experience negativity. Turn away from negativity anywhere it may be found. It takes two to argue. It takes a bigger, stronger person to turn away from an argument. If you find, yourself in an argument use the information contained in these pages to set yourself free. Because of your, knowledge you should naturally be the strongest one. Remember it's all what you are thinking about that will keep any argument alive. Words can soften the hardest heart. Words can inspire you and others to take action. Words can comfort you and others. Do your very, best to enhance your home with positive words. Positive words will generate positive good feelings. When your home, is enhance with positive energy this energy will be, reflected in the whole of your life. Everything you do will reflect your positive energy. Your positive energy will minimize disagreements in your household. If you have a disagreement in your household clear the air as soon as possible. Say or do something positive and happy as soon as possible.

You will notice the power of positive energy because your house will become a happy and better place. The key to, happy relationships is to simply refuse to think and feel negative, refuse to feel slighted, refuse to feel unimportant or insulted again. If you apply the information in these pages, they will transform your life. If you are in habitual emotional pain, you need something to stop the pain, something to stop you worrying and something to make you feel secure. You need to, realize that you are, thought manifested. Thought is involve in everything you do. Thought is responsible for the earth as it is and everything on it that includes you and me. Realize that you are thought also realize that no matter what you will be O.K. Yes, thought will always exist in various forms of energy. Modern science verifies that all that exists is energy in various forms. In time all energy changes, that change is what keeps the universe alive including our earth. In time, we all change to a different type of energy whether we like it or not we will change.

The natural inclination of humans is to be happy. Everything we do we do whit the hope of happiness from doing it. To that end many people get married or share their lives with, usually a member of the opposite sex in a romantic relationship. We think if we have someone to love and someone to love us back in return our lives would be happier.

Successful romantic love is built on, pure positive thoughts about the person, because that is what love is pure positive thoughts. When we love, someone we express that love positively by what we say and do. Yes your, love and happiness you have for a person or thing, is made evident by your emotional closeness. There are no, negative intentional thoughts or actions toward that person or thing you love. To continue to love someone habitual honest effort is needed to think positively about that person. It's by honestly thinking positively about the other person that we experience the full range of loving emotions and passion.

Anyone who controls his or her thought with Friendship with thought will be happy and prosperous in all situations. Because that is exactly what Friendship with thought produces, happy thoughts and feelings. Those feelings create conditions, that you take control of. You can always win more than you lose. You can, deliberately and consciously create any situation you choose. You already create all you situations every day as they are. Only now you; could use Friendship with thought, to consciously and deliberately create situations to your advantage. You can change any situation you choose just by thinking and seeing it differently, in a more friendly way. When you feel different to a particular situation, you will act in accordance with your feelings.

You can feel relaxed, calm, confident, contented, and happy anytime you choose. Just remember to apply Friendship with thought principles and you take control of your situation. Remember that you are always in a situation. Keep in mind that it's, your situations that give you your experiences. If people habitually think can't do negative low self-esteem thoughts that is exactly the situation they will find themselves in. That will be their exact experience of life, because our situations create our experiences. We create our situations with our thoughts, feelings, words and actions. The situations we create will deliver our experiences accordingly. If the situation you created is a happy situation, you will feel and act accordingly. If it is a negative situation, you will feel and act accordingly.

Whatever situation you create you will act and get the results accordingly. Thus, the situations you create will determine if you are predominantly happy or unhappy. Any situation you are in can change. You can remove yourself from any unwanted situation if you choose to do so. Alternatively, you can choose to take control of the situation by applying Friendship with thought principles in your life. Remember that you see people and things all as thoughts manifested. And that you are in control of your wonderful lovely thoughts in any situation you find yourself in. On the day you were born someone else were in control of you. Either your mother or someone else was in control. As the years went by if you did not consciously take responsibility and control of your thoughts then other people were continually in control of you.

You may have been habitually finding yourself in situations that you'd rather not be, all because of lack of control of your thoughts. If someone else is controlling your thoughts, you go and do as they say. Success or failure is dependent on the situation, you habitually find yourself in. Regular, habitual happy situations mean success. Regular habitual painful, stressful situations are indications that certain things are not going, as you want. In any stressful situation quickly take control of your thought, use Friendship with thought to take control. If you remain in those, type of situation they could easily drain your happy energy. You can easily identify positive or negative situations by the way they make you feel. You are happy and successful in every aspect of your life to the extent that you take control of your life. Happiness is the result of being positive in all situations. You know when you are happy, when the situation feels good, when the situation is right for you and the situation is valuable to you.

Habitual non-productive negative thoughts produces, negative non-productive feelings and situations. Those negative non-productive feelings and situations cut off productive conscious thoughts. Those habitual negatives, reduces people's positive efficient energy. With peoples positive efficiency energy cut off. They lack the drive, quality of life, well-being, self-worth and happiness. These happy qualities are so important to habitually, create wonderful qualities of life. It is more, conducive to happiness if we habitually create conditions which people love to continually, live in. Happy positive productive thoughts are the natural keys that link humans to all in existence. When apply in people lives Friendship with thought encourage, create and show people the way to habitual positive thoughts which result in a happier way of life.

Friendship with thought neutralizes all negative thoughts while at the same time replacing them with positive happy, confident thoughts. These thoughts, lets you carry on with your happy confident prosperous life. When you have only pure positive thoughts within you, you will have powerful control over all situations. You will have absolute certainty in all situations. You will know exactly what to do in all situations. You will know how to dissolve negative thoughts in yourself and in others. You will continue to hold the power of peace and prosperity in your thoughts. Keep in mind that you are always in a situation. Yes we are always in one situation after another, some familiar and some not so familiar. THE EASIEST, QUICKEST WAY TO FEEL HAPPY IS THROUGH PURE POSITIVE THOUGHTS AND ACTIONS. Yes, think and do something that will make you feel a bit better than you are currently feeling. This happy thinking and doing will change your state of being and you will change the situation.

With this knowledge and its implementation you are never frighten of any situation. That is because you always know that it is only a situation and you always know how to deal with it. If you are in a situation you do not like the feelings of notice your thoughts. Yes notice what you are currently thinking about the people and things involve in your situation. Change all negative thoughts about the situation. This change of thought will change how you feel about your current situation. Your changed feelings will change how you act towards your situation. Your positive action will change the situation, which will change your thoughts and feelings to a more pleasant happy state. Fearlessness allows you to take control. Living a pure habitual positive state gives a sense of being in control of your destiny. Of being in control in every aspect of you.

Pure positive thoughts of love for doing something, for a person or thing stimulates natural highs with no hang-over's, with no side effects. The ultimate natural high comes from being and feeling one's own true self-worth. How valuable to you do you habitually think you are? How useful to you do you habitually think you are? Natural highs also come from producing competitive tradable values for others. Of being in, control of your-self, in control of your situations, in control of your thoughts, in control of your life. Yes living a worry free life generates a natural high. Being in control allows you to be the boss. Being in control allows you to experience the best this world has to offer. Being in control allows you to go through life first class. To stay in control you need to maintain your positive optimistic outlook of life. By staying in control of you, you will experience the peace, prosperity, pleasures, happiness and satisfaction available from your life.

Keep in mind that your wonderful state of being is dependent on you releasing all habitual negative thoughts. Forget all thoughts that do not serve you. If any negative thoughts comes to mind, no matter what just acknowledge them then let them go. You may tend to want to justify negative thoughts don't, just let them go they are not adding to your happiness. Even if you justify them, they will not add to your happiness. By realising all, negative thoughts you free your mind and body to fully experience life at its best.

To enjoy the best that life has to offer you must have the confidence to want and importantly to do something to get the best. When you realize that everyone is a part of you, you are no longer afraid to do and be whatever or whoever you choose.

When you have the confidence to be and do as you please this boldness will result in prosperity and happiness on an ascending scale. I will remind you that the message in this book is you can do have or be whatever or who-ever, you choose. Yes you can easily, almost effortless, as if by magic, as if by coincidence have what you want. You can be who, you choose to be and have whatever you choose to have.

Believe in your-self you are here this very moment. You are always in a particular situation. Believe in your-self to handle any situation you are in. If you are from a poor background you can change your situation, you do not have to stay poor all your life. You can change from a poor background to a wealthy way of life. To succeed in anything you do you need courage and confidence. Your courage and confidence can, be built even stronger than they are at this moment. Confidence is a type of being sure. Are you sure that you are alive? Are you confident that you are alive? If you are absolutely, certain that you are alive then you can take that thought and feeling of absolutely certainty and confidence into any situation and display those qualities.

You can make the thought and feeling of certainty become your dominant state. The use of Friendship with thought will give you the energy and power to be confident. When you are confident you feel at ease and are sure of your ability ability to do whatever you think will make you happy. We have all made mistakes, face the fact of your mistake.

Face the fact that you have made certain mistakes which if you could you would undo. You have made mistakes, which if the same situation arises; you have no intention of repeating or experiencing again. You may have enjoyed what you did or did not do. However, because of the feelings it created in you after you have no intention, of repeating it. You can create the energy to do whatever it takes, for you to succeed.

Energize yourself to succeed with powerful graceful thoughts. Remember that, Good or bad, positive or negative, pleasurable or painful we create the situations that cause everything to happen in our lives. The fact that you are a part of the situation means that you had a part in creating it. If you were not there you would not be part of the situation, you would not have had that experience. You did not become the person who you are overnight. You build your personality, your attitude and your way of life a little at a time. It pays to be auspicious. When you are, ready another helper will appear in your life to take you further into your wonderful awareness. Your helper can be in the form of another book or a human. Take on an identity that will make you happy, an identity that is acceptable to you.

Enjoy the present and always look forward to the future because here is where you will meet up with your happiness. Your hope is in the future, but your life can only be enjoy in the present wherever you are. If for any reason you are turn down be aware that out of this can come better opportunities.

Positivity helps us to deal with the difficulties of life. Be someone that others have a need for. On your journey through life if your path is block simply make a detour; go around it or them. Patience always pays off. Keep in mind that we set our own limits, our own benchmark, and our own parameters. Your prosperity is, limited only by the benchmark that defines the parameters of your own way of life. Each of us sees the same person and situations differently, according to what we think of them.

DUALITY AND CHOICES

The natural law of duality gives us our choices. The law of duality states that there is always an opposite. From this law we have two choices. From this law people make all of their life's choices. You do everything you do because of the choices you make. You are who you are because of the choices you have made. Everything you have is because of the choices you have made. Duality means that it will happen, that it must happen. You are either, in good health or you are sick. You are either hot or cold. You are either rich or poor. By rich, I mean that you do not have any worry or fear about money because you have more than enough to meet your responsibilities. By poor, I do not mean that you are starving, but you are not rich you are always in need of more money. You can choose happiness or pain, wealth or poverty. You can choose productivity or laziness. You can choose easy or hard. You can choose to be predominantly positive or predominantly negative. That is the law of duality. It is simply a matter of choice between two choices. You choose what you want or what you want to be. You will make a choice to act on the information contain in this book or not. Deliberately or unwittingly, you will make a choice. Consciously or unwittingly, we all make choices and we get the results accordingly.

It all comes down to simply choosing as simple and easy as that. When you know it, it becomes ever so easy. Without knowing that it is simply a choice people put all sorts of limitations and conditions on themselves. Even now, I suspect that you may be saying it cannot be that easy. I say to you to test it out in objective reality start by making a deliberate choice to only think and use positive words. Positive thoughts and negative thoughts have electromagnetic poles. Positive and negative thoughts are magnetic with opposite poles. When you are positive you will naturally think, say and do positive things you feel good. Positive thoughts will generate positive feelings and will attract positive people and things to you by what you say and do. Positive thoughts are, like a magnetic field and will protect you from habitual negative people and negative situations. When you are, negative nothing seems to be going your way and you feel low. If you find that you are always struggling, always fighting life, notice what you are thinking. Chances are that you are thinking or saying something negative.

Words can change you. It depends on the type of words you choose to use or the type of words you listen to. Positive words can change you for the better. Positive information can change you for the better. Positive knowledge can change you; make you see people and things differently in a more friendly happy light. When you see people and things in a positive light, you will behave positively towards them. Likewise negative words, information or knowledge can change you. Negativity makes people behave towards each other in hostile manners. Words, information and knowledge are powers that change your thoughts and feelings.

Thoughts, words, information and knowledge are powers that create your emotional energy, your feelings. Having this knowledge puts in a position of choice. You can choose to use predominantly positive words, information and knowledge in your everyday activities. If you choose, to use predominant positivity in your life you will in a short while notice, the happy differences. Deliberately choose positivity you have nothing to lose by choosing to use predominantly positive thoughts and words. The whole of, our life is based on choices. Big or small, your choice will determine your future. It is all choices. People make important choices without the knowledge of this natural law. Consequently, many people are living in the dark unaware of this natural law when it comes to making important choices. Continuous positive thoughts will deliver those wonderful people and things as part of your life. We will do what we continuously think, about. If you continuously, think positive things you will do positive things and get the results accordingly. If you continuously think negative things you will do negative things and will get the results accordingly.

Your joy, prosperity, wealth, peace and happiness all depends on the choices you make. When people do not know about this law, they make hit and miss choices. Little wonder why so many people are dissatisfied and unhappy with their lot in life. If you choose to ignore this natural, law or leave your choices up to blind chance. You will continue to make haphazard choices and get haphazard results. It does not have to be that way. If you choose to put this law to work in your life then the sky is your limit. You become a limitless being when it comes to choosing things that will make you happy. Your learnt decision to make conscious positive choices will become your natural inclination. This natural inclination of habitually choosing exactly what will make you happy irrespective of price will open the doors of prosperity to you. These natural laws and principles when applied will make your doing to get what you want much easier and faster than your old previous ways of doing to get the things you want. When you feel happy to do whatever you want to do, you will be happy to do it. Your continuous positive happy thoughts are what drive you to accomplish anything you want to accomplish.

When you want, something or you want to do something you will have to think about it a while in advance. A little while, before you actually have it in objective reality or doing what you want to experience. Completely forget about the price, if you think about the price, you may limit yourself from having what you want. If you think, about the price you may talk yourself out of what you want to have or what you want to do. This natural law will permeate all area of our life. This will enable you to do whatever is necessary to live a wonderful, happy limitless life to the full. Yes that wonderful life that you want and have chosen to live. As humans our most wanted of all things is happiness.

When you are, secure you are happy. With making, the right choices you will naturally create lasting security, peace, prosperity and happiness. This includes the choice to use the Principle of Friendship with thought in your everyday life. When these natural laws and principles in this book becomes your natural way of thinking and living then every door of opportunity in all situations is open to you. It is your new positive confident way of thinking that will create and open all doors of opportunities to you.

It will all become only matters of choices. Keep in mind that you must do something in order to make your dreams come true. Only now, you will find doing almost effortless. You will look forward to do because you are consciously choosing what you want to do. You have the choice of staying at the same level of life or you can choose to upgrade your life to the highest level. That is the choice before you, your choice. You have the ability, capability and choice to exceed all your previous levels of accomplishments. A key to unlocking your limitless potential is to understand what you have learned to think and feel about yourself. In the light of what you are learning now if what you have learned to think about yourself in the past was mainly negative you can change those thoughts. If you understand, that it is your patterns of thoughts that have kept you at your present level of life. This understanding will allow you to choose new ways of thinking and behaving. Your new thoughts; will result in more positive feelings about you. You can now, choose to consciously and deliberately think predominantly positive thoughts about you.

The choice to exert positive thoughts and effort or giving into non-productive laziness determines what type of life you will create. The simple childlike choice between choosing to be predominantly productive or being lazier and non-productive determines people happiness and prosperity or lack and poverty. Laziness is contagious. Laziness is like, a contagious disease that insidiously infect a person without them quite being aware that they are infected. You may be, infected with the disease of laziness without you not being fully aware if you are. Be careful of getting too close to people with the disease of laziness less they infect you with their lazier disease. Laziness all starts in the mind, with people's choices of habitual thoughts.

When people default on their obligations and responsibilities it becomes easy for them to adopt a, can't do mentality. Once the dieses of the lazy dependency mentality is; adopted and developed, the host who is infected will fight tooth and nail to hold onto their personality, their attitude and their identity. Keep in mind that this disease affect; people mentality it affects their way of thinking. They become afraid to change their beliefs, they are afraid to change their attitude and they are afraid to change their personality. That way of thinking becomes their way of life. People then pass on this, dieses to others for generations, usually to members of their own family, without quite realising that they are infecting other people with this deadly dieses. To live a full and happy life people must, need to cure themselves of the dieses of laziness. How? By, using Friendship with thought. Keep in mind that everything starts with your thought.

By becoming fearless, and happy to "do" you will do. When we are, fearless and happy to do we will do. When we are fearless and happy to do, we will go where no man has gone before. When we are fearless and happy to do, we will do what no man has done before and much more. With fearlessness and happiness even if, that doing is to climb Mt Everest, to sail single handily around the world or any other challenge we will do it. When you are, cured of, your fears of doing, you will be a fearless get-up and do person.

When you are happy with doing, you will do anything you want. Yes to do people must get rid of all of their subconscious fears. Your subconscious fears are thoughts of fear that you are not quite aware of. You may not even realize that you have certain fears that are limiting you. You may have certain subconscious fears that are stopping you from doing or having certain things. Those fears you may have picked up as a child, which became parts of your beliefs. Remember that we are compelled to behave, to act according to our beliefs. Consciously or subconsciously, we will act according to our beliefs.

If you have any types of conscious or subconscious negative limiting beliefs you will be compelled to act according to those beliefs.

Happiness comes from doing, from producing competitive values for others. When you provide competitive values for others, you automatically provide happiness for yourself. You like me want to be happy. We all create situations and expectations that deliver our experiences of life. When you create situations and expectations of happiness that is exactly what you will experience. There are two types of expectations, negative and positive expectations. Negative expectations are to habitually expecting others to do for you what only you can do for yourself. Avoid habitually expecting others to take away your fears and to live your life for you. Positive expectations are you will do your best and expect things to turn out according to your best or better. There are two types of dependencies. Negative dependencies are habitually depending on the approval of others, the acceptance of others for your happiness and success. Positive dependencies are relying on your-self and do whatever you know you can do to make you happy.

To change you must be willing to change. If people are unwilling to change in the face of new information, new knowledge they will remain stock as they are. Life is about growth and expansion. Emotional growth and expansion do not just automatically happen in people they must search for what they want.

People must look for what makes them happy. To give up searching for what you think will trigger happiness in you is to give up on life. Anything or anyone that will help to change your old attitude, character and personality and how you view and interpret the world and your situations should worth your time and effort. When you find what you are looking for, it will make all effort you put in worth your while. If you are aware of any negative thoughts about your search, change them as soon as possible. A fearless attitude to live in happy situations will produce more of the same. You will do, and be anyone and anything you choose with a fearless personality.

People become happy, powerful, prosperous, and secure by fearlessly being themselves. By, being who they choose to be. With their fearless personality, attitude and beliefs powerful people ignore negative things what others may say or think about them. These fearless people proudly work and produce happy competitive values in any way. Where there is no fear there is no pain. Being fearless in all situations is pure positive living and creating your life of well-being. We all have two important basic choices when it comes to thoughts. We can create predominantly positive thoughts or negative thoughts. Most people exercise these choices unwittingly, that is to say they are not quite aware of making those choices on a daily basis. The removal of habitual predominant negative thoughts is the cure all. Sad, angry, worrying, painful thoughts do not exist when you are happy, they just would not be. Predominantly positive thoughts result in states of habitual happiness. Is learning to create predominantly positive thoughts worth your time?

Can you imagine the large majority of your thoughts, feelings, and actions being only pure positives thoughts? What do you think the results of your life would be? Keep in mind that our thoughts; create our feelings and actions? With continuous pure positive thoughts, you would be amongst the happiest people on earth. The reason for this happy state is we must all think, feel and do; we never stop thinking feeling and doing. So if the majority of your thoughts, feelings and the things you do is positive this, will be reflected in your life accordingly. Yes when you remove all negative thoughts you will be, left with pure positive thoughts. This will take practice and getting used to eventually you will be that way.

You created the life you are living at this very moment that way, most likely subconsciously. How long it takes to, consciously create your new life is entirely dependent on you. It depends how much quality time you are prepared to put in to change. This can be fun, so make it so every day. You already have the most important thing to succeed in anything you want. Yes, you already, have what it takes to succeed; only you are not quite sure about what you have. Every person who have ever succeed, who have ever wanted great power, great wealth and great reaches and got them have exactly what you have. They all had themselves yes they all had them-selves. Without them-self, success would be impossible. You have you, without you, success would be impossible. Yes you have the most important thing for success, you. Without you, the universe does not exist. Without you planet Earth does not exist. Without you the most valuable the most useful things you currently want has no meaning. Without you nothing, matters. That is how important you are. You have a clean slate choose who and what you want to be and start being that person. No one except you can stop you from being who you what to be. Friendship with thought is a necessity to live peaceful, calm prosperous lives. Keep in mind that your experiences are your reality, your life.

Happiness; is created in many different ways. One of the main ways happiness is, created is by creating competitive values for others. When you create, competitive value for others you automatically create values for yourself. What you think about those values create either happiness or sadness in you. If you accept that, then you will understand to; a large extent it is what or who you think about that triggers happiness or sadness in you. Therefore, happiness is positive thoughts about someone or something. If this is true then no thoughts should stand in your way of success and happiness. You have control of your thoughts so you can think exactly what you wish and choose to think. It is only a matter of practicing your new way of thinking. As I have mentioned before installing your new personality is as easy as breathing. Use The Breath Method to help create your new personality. You can choose to think about people and things differently, in a more upbeat way, when you think of them that way you feel good.

Worry is a negative thought about someone, something or about tomorrow. If you want to be happy stop worrying you cannot run out of happy thoughts. If you know, for absolute certainty that you cannot run out of happiness what will you think? What would you do? When you are, happy good happy things happen. Happiness is a state of mind. Happiness is creates when you think something pleasant about someone or something. When you do something, say something or have something that makes you feel good this will result in happiness. In a happy state people, and things all appears to be OK. In a happy state, all is well. All will continue to be well for as long as you maintain your happy state. Everyone and everything are representations of thoughts. There will always be high and low states of mind and being. From this principle, we make our choices as to what we will make our dominant state.

If you want, to be predominantly happy do not stay too long in a low state, no matter what caused that state. Happiness can be your continuous way of being your life is worth it. By being aware of the principle of duality and understanding that there will always be an opposite. You can use this principle to your advantage. As I have mentioned above the secret is not to stay in any low negative state. Once you recognize that you are in a low state of mind find ways to change that state. The first place to start is to stop thinking about what has triggered that low state. The second thing to do is to find someone or something you love or like that will make you feel happy when you think about them. Continue to think about that person or thing that makes you feel happy and you have changed your low state. To maintain your happy state find something positive to do so as you do it you will feel happier. Your moods determine your experiences of life.

Your mood will change sometimes you will feel high and sometimes you will feel low. The important thing to remember is that mood swings are natural parts of life. There will always be high and there will always be low moods. The key is to manage your moods effectively for your happiness and well-being. Some people when, they are in a low mood eat or drink alcohol, be careful with this type of diversion. The reason for being careful with using food and alcohol as pain relief is. You could use food or alcohol to overcome one type of pain while creating another type of pain that potentially could be worse than the first pain. If you habitually, use food or alcohol as pain relief you could find yourself overeating or over drinking alcohol to the point where you become addictive to them.

What people have and do are all representations of their thoughts. The life you live, your life-style is a representation of your thoughts. If you want to change your life, you must first change your old thoughts. Habitually think of the person you want to be. Habitually think happy thoughts about the things you will like to do and have. Those happy thoughts will become part of whatever you want to do. They will give you the energy to; gradually start doing whatever you choose to do. You will find it easy to do them with these happy feelings in you. Keep in mind that if you don't think about it; it won't happen your way. You must regularly think about it to create the energy for it to happen, as you want it to be.

Once you have the happy energy of it in you, consciously or subconsciously you will do things to make it happen your way. Make the thought of whatever you want to do positive. When your thought, of what you want to do is happy, doing becomes happy. Remember that there is no fear or pain where there is happiness. Confidence; belong to those who are brave enough to use it, be confident and use your happy positive thoughts and feelings to do and have whatever you want. I know you will have to get use to this positive way of thinking, once you get used to it; it is yours it becomes your new way of thinking. You can be the person you choose to be, a person you love and admire and like being with.

Have you notice that some people appear to succeed without trying hard. Usually these type; of people have a quiet confidence about them. People sense their confidence and thrust success upon them. These naturally quiet confident people do not have to try hard because they have what it takes to succeed. They acquire this confidence either through deliberately learning to be confident as you are doing now. Alternatively, they acquire their confidence by being in a predominant positive environment. Either way that confidence is part of them and they naturally act accordingly. Be aware of how, you want to see yourself and be seen by others. If you leave, it too chance it would not happen the way you want it to be. Keep in mind that you are in the process of building your new personality and attitude. This building process includes rejection all negative thoughts and beliefs about you.

Your confidence comes from your positive thoughts about yourself in relation to people and things. Do not be overly concern about what other people may be thinking about you. Forget what you think other people may or may not be thinking about you. You need to and must think positive happy things about you to have high self-esteem. Your habitual positive high esteem about you is more important to you than what others may think or say about you. Your confidence is your willpower and your drive to do whatever you want to do. It; is only fear or pain that is keeping people from achieving their heart desires. We all have some confidence. We are all confident in some things. To build your confidence even stronger in certain areas think happy positive thoughts about those particular areas. For example if you are about to give a presentation or performance think positive important things about what you are about to say or do.

Realize that what you are about to do or about to say is important. Realize that what you are about to say or do is of value to you as well as to others. Others may say or do what you are about to say or do differently, that's fine they are not you. You do or say what you have to do or say your way and others do or say theirs their way. When you think happy thoughts, you will feel happy and comfortable about your performance. With your wonderful high confidence, you will go on and give your best. With high self-esteem, you can do anything you want.

The law of duality gives us our choices. Happiness is a choice, being rich is a choice. Sadness is a choice; living in poverty is a choice. Consciously or subconsciously, people made those choices to stay in certain situation or to move on. You may ask how about those people who were born in poverty. I will answer they can choose to take appropriate action to come out of poverty. The fact that they do not have the knowledge or information that is required to take themselves, out of poverty they remain subconscious in poverty. With the correct; information or knowledge they can choose to use that knowledge to take themselves out of poverty. No matter where you look in the world among any group of people you will always find there are some who are doing better than the rest. People can look and find a way if they so choose. The sad thing about living in poverty is that people get used to poverty and accept it as a way of life. Consciously or subconsciously, people stay in their situation for various reasons. Being rich or, being poor is a choice all-be it in most instances a subconscious choice. Happiness or sadness; is a choice like riches or poverty in most instances is chosen subconsciously.

Other people cannot think for you. You have the ability and freedom of what to choose to think about you. What you think, about your-self you are the one who is doing the thinking. You can choose to think positive things about your-self. You can also choose to think negative things about yourself and you will feel and act accordingly. Positive of negative you will experience the feelings of your thoughts and actions. You can choose to have high self-esteem for your-self. You can choose to create high positive regards toward yourself. It is your responsibility and duty to think positive things about you. What others think about you that's their thoughts. People in general do not have positive high regards for themselves. To succeed in whatever you want you need to change your current self-image around that which you want. You need to change how you see yourself in relation to your wants. You need to think and see yourself positively in relation to your wants. Until your self-image, around the things change there is no point in trying to achieve them. If you do not think you are worth them no matter how hard you try you will be subconsciously be pushing them away from you then call it bad luck. If you do not change all negative thoughts, about the things you want. Situations will appear to conspire against you to bring them out of your reach and you will put it down to bad luck. While all the while, it is because of your negative thoughts about things you want in relation to you that is pushing them away. You are the one who is unwittingly pushing them away without quite being aware that you are doing so. When you think, positive thoughts about the things you want there are no fears. Where there is no fear there is confident. When you are, confident you will take action to do what you must do to achieve your wants. TO ACHIEVE ANYTHING YOU WANT YOU NEED TO THINK POSITIVELY ABOUT IT AND TAKE POSITIVE ACTION TOWARD IT.

To have high, self-esteem for your-self you must create those, high self-esteem thoughts for your-self. The current self-image you have is your beliefs about you. Your self-image is made up of beliefs such as, who you think you are. What you think you deserve and how much you believe you should spend on you. We are not only talking about money. We are also talking about good feelings, time and attention for you. Honestly answer this question, how much do you honestly think you should spend on you? Keep in mind that there is only one you. How valuable is, you to you? For the moment suspend what you believe or think others may think about you. It is what, you think about you that really matters. I once again ask you, how valuable is you to you? The reality is, without you nothing else matters. That's how important you are.

Your; current beliefs about yourself are the result of the repeated messages you heard, gave yourself, and accepted in your past. These messages in most instances are mainly subconscious thoughts about you in relation to the world around you. As a child, you received instructions from others in authority. You believed most of these, instruction without question and these instructions have shaped your personality and attitude up until now. Some of the things you were thought as a child may not have been facts, however if you believed them they would have shape the person who you are today. For example, as a child you may have been told that the dead; can harm you. Consequently, you grew up being terrify of the dead and all sorts of limiting negative beliefs about the dead. You may have, been told that people of a certain nationality are all rich only to find out that there are rich and poor people in every nation.

We have all, been programmed by our past. It is our; programming that makes us believe certain things and to behave in certain ways and to take certain action. It is all down to what you have inside of you, yes the type of thoughts you have in you. The image you create in your mind about yourself will determine the person you will be, because you will believe that image and act accordingly. You will always find evidence to support your personality and attitude you have developed as your way of life. The evidence you get will justify why something is possible or not for you. With high self-esteem, all things are possible. With positive self-image, all things are possible. To regard your-self highly is to; always wish the best for your-self.

If you are, not happy with your life as it is you can change it. To have your life, as you want you need to create an image of the person you want to be. Your, self-image is the foundation upon which your life is built. Yes, you built your life according to who you believe you are. You built your own self-image. You may have, been influenced by others but you built your own self-image. You were not born the way you currently are; you were not born with your current attitude and personality. You were not born with those qualities you currently have. You were not born with the beliefs you currently hold. You adopted your beliefs, your attitude and your personality as you travelled along life's road. You can consciously and deliberately change your self-image if you so wish. Your childhood beliefs that you have programmed into you may not be serving you. If you notice, that you are not getting what you want out of life you will need to change some of your childhood thoughts. You need to reprogram those thoughts and beliefs that hold you back. You are free to change your beliefs about anything in the light of new evidence.

You create a new positive image of you by habitually thinking about how you want to be. You continuously think, about the type of life you want to live. It is exactly, that way you have created your current image of yourself. You most likely created this image of yourself unwittingly without fully realizing that you were doing so. Consequently, you may have installed all sorts of unwanted fears that continually hold you back from doing things that will make you happier. Never the less you and you alone created your self-image. Keep in mind that you can change your current self-image and self esteem if you so choose to. If you want, a more happy life, a more prosperous life, a more abundant life, a more successful life; then you must habitually see yourself as such. You can create your new self-image as you wish by continually and habitually thinking about how you want to be and the life, you want to live. You will soon find that you get use to thinking, feeling and doing your new way of life. You will have created your new comfort zone. You will shortly feel comfortable with your new identity. You will feel comfortable doing things according to your new personality.

Keep on thinking and doing your new ways of life and in a short while you will be living your new way of life. Keep in mind that as you keep thinking and doing according to your new way of life internal changes are taking place in you. These internal changes will manifest themselves in objective reality by the new things you do or don't do as the case may be. You may decide to stop certain practices or certain things. You may decide to start doing certain things that you have always wanted to until now. Remember that our thoughts manifest themselves in the material world. Keep on thinking about the people and things you want as part of your life. Keep on thinking about the experiences you would like to have. Everything, you do or have are manifestations of thoughts. The whole world is a manifestation of thoughts. Make sure that you do want those changes that you think about. Because you will, do things in line with your thoughts to bring about changes in your life. You will, soon become comfortable and accustom to your new changes. They will become your new way of life.

For you to be what you want you must debatably create the person you want to be rather than leaving it to chance. Yes, you must do something positive to be and to have whatever you want. Use Friendship with thought to help you change your thoughts about people and things. When you change, your thoughts about someone or something you automatically change how you feel about that person or thing. When you change, your feelings about someone or something you will change how you act towards that person or thing. Keep in mind that our thoughts create our feelings and our feelings create our actions.

If you leave, your personality and attitude change to chance your subconscious will continue to give you more of what you are uses to. You can be confident that it is possible for you to make any change you choose. Yes, it is possible for you to make changes. You can be confident that you can change your personality and attitude. For you to change and become who you want to be you need to habitual think about the way you want to live. Imagine yourself doing the things you really want to do. Picture yourself having the things you really want to have. At this stage, forget about how much money it will cost. If you think, mainly about the cost you are likely to talk yourself out of what you want. Think mainly about the things you want. The true cost to anything we want is our positive thoughts and feelings about what we want. If you really want something don't tell yourself that it's too expensive just habitually think about it. And feel how it will feel to have the attention of your thought in objective reality.

When you picture someone or something as far as your subconscious is concern it is real. That is why you feel the way you feel about it when you see it. Remember that it's not so much the money it cost but rather it is what you believe about that person or thing in relation to yourself. It is what you think and feel about that person or thing in relation to yourself. Habitually think and feel how it feels to have the things you really what. By thinking, feeling and picturing yourself doing what you really want your subconscious mind will soon adopt your new way of life. Once your subconscious has adopted your new way of life you will believe that is your way of life and you will behave accordingly. You will naturally live according to your habitual thoughts. You will live according to what you believe your new way of life to be. Once you have a strong healthy self-image of the person you want to be in place then you will act accordingly. With a strong self-image of who you are everything else become easier and more straightforward because that is the way you will be living your life.

The fact that you have reached this stage in you change and development you are well on your way, removing all unnecessary difficulties and struggles from your life. Gone is the old personality with its limiting beliefs, self-doubts and habitual struggles. In come your new positive happy personality and attitude. By creating your new self-image you will have automatically replace your old personality with your new personality and attitude. Your new attitude and personality is one of quiet confidence, one of action one of success and one of ease.

HAPPINESS

Happiness is a pleasant way of thinking and a pleasant type of feeling. To be happy and to stay happy think positively about what you have more often than, what you do not have.

As humans we, are on the hunt, the search, the quest for happiness. Everything we do the bottom line is for happiness. Being aware of your purpose for doing what you do will help you do the right things more often than not. When you are aware that you are doing what you are doing to make yourself and possible others happy you will be more likely to be happy doing what you are doing. If you are happy to do something chances are, you will do it. Before discovering positive thinking, I used to think that my success and happiness depended on other people. I now know it is; the individual that must create their own happiness by what they think and do. You are an individual you have to be who you want to be no one can be you for you.

People will help you thus far; the rest is up to you. Your positive thoughts about people and things will help create your happiness. The positive knowledge you have will help create your happiness. The positive information you receive will create your happiness. Your positive thoughts, knowledge, information and the positive things you do will see you through. Our expectations can make us happy or sad; you can do things to expect happy results. Keep in mind that the bottom line for us humans is happiness. You deserve to live your life to the full; you deserve to be predominantly happy. The fact that you are alive as a human automatically gives you that right to be happy.

When you share, your happiness with others you expand your own happiness. When you do, something good today that good will result in good today and in happy memories tomorrow. By good I mean absolutely anything that makes you and others feel good without causing any harm. What you do does not necessarily have to be something big. Quite often it; is the little packages that contain the most precious things. Your, happiness is created from you freedom to do and have whatever you choose. Freedom comes from knowing that no matter what everything will be O.K. Freedom comes from expressing your thoughts. This freedom can be express in countless ways. Being creative in your way of life is being free. You have the freedom to express your thoughts, your opinions. You express your thoughts by what you say and do. You can express your thoughts as a painter, a musician, a poet, a cook, a pilot, a sculptor or any other means you choose. Yes to live your thoughts; that is the reason you are alive, to express your thoughts and opinions in various ways. If you let other people, they will take this freedom away from you in the guises of religion or politics. Your freedom is worth every effort of yours to safeguard it. Protect your freedom no matter what else you do with your life; your freedom is worth it. The service of others brings all sorts of benefits including freedom. If you are focused on others well-being you are free from any fear that may hinder you. Concern for others, takes away the fears and leave you free to deliver happiness to others. I would like you to keep in mind the importance of choices. Remember that everything you do and have is a result of the choices you have made. The more right choices you make is the happier your life will be. To help you make more right choices than otherwise just be aware as much as possible of the choices you make. Do your best to see where your choices will lead you. If you think the choice you are about to make will result in your happiness without causing any harm then be conscious and go right ahead and make your choice.

YOUR LIMITLESS MONEY

Money, makes the world go round, yes money makes the world work. Take a look around you it is very likely that everything around you cost money. Without money the world would stop, such is the power and importance of money. Without money, our world would change completely. For the world to function without money humans would have to go way back in time. For the world to work without money humans would have to change their mentality completely. We would have to change the way we think about everyone and everything. Money is a part of each and every-one of us life's today. Having enough or large, sums of money makes you think a certain way. Money makes you feel a certain way. With large sums of money, people feel secure and confident. Without money, people say and do things they otherwise would not have said or done if they had enough money.

Money gives us hope for a better tomorrow. Money makes it possible to move from one lifestyle to another. Large sums of money, gives us a sense of security and a feeling of confidence and pride. People are attracted to money for various reasons. Money sets us free. Money breaks the chains of poverty. Pure positive thoughts about money make it possible to have as much money as you choose.

However with your, pure positive thoughts must come action. You must do something to make your dream of having large sums of money become a reality. If you take, a look at rich successful people they all have two things in common. They all "SELL" something. They all give something for a price. They all offer something at a profit and they all have the energy to "do".

The difference between these successful people and the not so successful people is they are not afraid to "do". They have the confidence, the power and the energy of "DOING". They find doing easier than most people do. They can DO anything they want. You also can develop the will to do. You can use Friendship with thought to help you develop your confidence to achieve anything you want. You are either confident or are afraid. If you are, confident you are not afraid and you; will also have the power of doing. Your every action springs from your thoughts. Everything you do and have is a result of your thought. You are either afraid to do or say something or you are confident to do or say what you really want to. By thinking of thought as one entity manifested in countless ways you too can have the confidence to do and have whatever you what.

When you think of thought as one entity, you know that you are, connected to everyone and everything because everyone and everything are all thoughts manifested in various forms. Look in objective reality and you will notice this to be true. If you are, afraid to do something you are being afraid of your thoughts. If you think, someone or something is too good for you; you are thinking that, that thought is too good for you. They are not too good for you because everything and everyone are thought; manifested just like you. You will need to get used to this way of thinking. When you do, you can do anything you want. When you do, you can have as much money as you want. By using Friendship with thought, you will dissolve all fears that stop you from taking action. Remember that fears are negative thoughts that we create our selves. Pure positive thoughts about people and things are a natural way of life to gain limitless wealth. When you have pure positivity about yourself, people and things you are confident, you are not afraid.

When you are, confident you have the power to do anything you want to do. Money gives its owner power to do or have almost anything humanly possible. Pure positive thought about money is an easy way to gain limitless power and wealth. By accepting Friendship with thought as your way of life, you automatically put an end to all negative thoughts and hurts. That includes putting an end to all hurtful thoughts about money. You also put an end to all those unnecessary worries and setbacks that have habitually kept you from becoming the person you have always dreamed of being. It is your state, the mood you are in, that determines the quality of your situation and what you will do and have. It's your situations that, counts because from your situation you have and do everything in your life.

From your situations, you get your life's experiences. You can control your situation thus controlling what comes into your life including money.

The concept of Friendship with thought gives its owner great power to do, to become who they want to become. The concept has at its base, its core habitual pure positive thoughts as a way of life. Yes no matter, who no matter what always keep in mind that everything and everyone springs from thought. You are who you are today because of the things that you have thought and done until now. Your wealth or poverty are results of what you habitually think and do. By fully understanding, this law you will become a person that know with absolute certainty and fearlessness that you yourself is who makes your life as it is. Such an individual becomes a most important and powerful person. Keep in mind that money is, attached to every single person and everything in our world.

Some people say that money can't buy happiness I say to such people think again. I say to such people look around and you will notice the number of separations and devoices mainly because of a lack of money. I am not saying that money is the only cause I am saying that in a large number of separations and devoices a lack of money is at the bottom of them. With enough money, people can easily solve most of their problems. Positive thoughts about, money will energizes you to want to have large sums of money. If you allow negative thoughts about money to be your dominant thoughts you will be a part of the unhappy world of negative thinkers. If that is so unless you change your thoughts about money, you will always be in lack of money because you have made that your dominant thoughts. The simple fact is we create our world with our dominant thoughts.

Negativity not only affects people financial situation, if encourage negativity will permeate every area of people lives. People develop a way of thinking and they become comfortable with it. It becomes a way of life for them. They create unnecessary problems when none exists. Habitual problems becomes like an additive drug for them including thoughts about not having enough money. They must have their daily fix of problems. They can just as easily have their daily fix of happiness if only they knew about Friendship with thought. Friendship with thought results in happiness.

Before discovering Friendship with thought I subconsciously passed on predominant negative cannot do thoughts and negative not good enough low self-esteem, thoughts to my family. I used to think that certain things, places and activities were not for me. I used to think, that large sums of money was not for me, for others, but not for me. That I; was not good enough to have or do certain things. In addition, that the wonderful lovely things of this world were reserve for only certain type of people. I had in my world-view and my subconscious that large sum of money was not for me, for someone else but not for me. When I discovered Friendship with thought and started to think, feel, link and see everyone and everything including myself, and money as thoughts manifested my whole life changed for the better. This change of attitude and personality does not suddenly happen. It will take a little while to develop your new personality.

Once you develop your new predominantly positive personality, your attitude will change automatically accordingly. Keep in mind that money is a thought manifested. Money; was made by humans. Just as this book you are now reading, all are thoughts manifested. Develop the attitude that you are worthy, yes deserving and valuable enough to have and own large sums of money. When you know that you are, connected to everyone and everything and that everyone and everything are just the same as you, you are no longer afraid. You are not afraid of yourself are you? If you are, remember that we are, just one big thought manifested in various forms. When you do, you are no longer afraid; you become link to everyone and everything. In your fearless, state you become confident and super productive.

People need to continually think about things that; will make them happy. If they think otherwise, they will do and get the results of their thoughts. That's the way we are made we do and get what we most think about.

It's out thoughts and feelings toward that person or thing that we value most, even if most people are not quite aware of this fact. All value exist in relation to thoughts and feelings, especially so to the individual. When you want something to be part of your life, forget about the cost, forget about how much money you will have to pay for it. Think about the experience of having it instead of the price of it. Think about the wonderful experience of having it or the experience of doing it. If you continually dwell on the price of it, you may talk yourself out of it.

Everyone and everything are thoughts manifested including you. The fact that thoughts are, linked to all that exist including you and money means that you are automatically worthy to experience any thought unless you think it otherwise. Yes you are worthy of anyone, anything or any thought that would make you happy including large sums of money. If you habitually think, consciously or unwittingly that you are not worthy to experience whatever you would like to experience that is exactly what your life would reflect. You will not experience those lovely things because you are habitually thinking that you are not worthy to experience them. If that is your habitual thoughts, stop thinking that way. You are telling yourself that you are not worthy to experience them so you won't if you continue telling yourself that. Consciously and habitually tell yourself that you are worthy of the best of things, and of large sums of money. Notice what you are habitually imagining. Remember that people, become and see what's in their thoughts, we see what we expect.

Keep in mind, that thoughts create objective reality; yes, all there are is manifestations of thoughts including money. To prosper value your thoughts, make your thoughts valuable to yourself and others. Creation of valuable, joyful, happy, thoughts leads to increase happiness, wealth, riches and more prosperity in all areas of life. Self worth are thoughts about the individual, no one can create your thoughts of self worth for you. People may be able to influence your thoughts if you let them but no one can create your thoughts for you.

Self-worth and happiness must be, created by the individual by you. When people create, positive thoughts about people and things and them-self they increase their positivity. They increase their self-worth, happiness, money, and prosperity. They increase their, well-being and they flourish easily. Do your best to remember that everything is linked to money including, you. Look in objective reality and you will see this to be true. In order to prosper we need to stay loyal to pure positive thoughts about ourselves other people and things. You and you alone hold the right to decide, to say what you are good enough to own or do, no matter what, that right, that power belong to you. Keep in mind that thought and feelings are energies.

The real value to what we want is our happy thoughts and feelings about what we want. You could live in a wonderful palace however if you think little of it; it would not make you feel happy. If you live in that wonderful palace and had negative thoughts about it that palace would not trigger happiness in you. It is your happy thoughts about what you have, that counts. These are the real value not the price tag on the object. It's your, thoughts and feelings that are the real value. When you feel wonderful, about it that means that you value it greatly. If you do not have a wonderful feeling about it that means you are not much interested in it.

What you think and how you feel about the object of your attention is the price you must pay including how you feel about money. Yes, you pay for your money by how you feel about it. So, if you think the price is too high you may not buy the object, you are thinking about.

There are countless ways to own something. If you think and feel wonderful about it and continue to feel wonderful about it, that object will come into your possession. You will do and say things to bring the object of your thought to you. Our properties are extensions of our thoughts, including money, every-thing you own and do are extensions of you. How much you have is how much you honestly think you deserve. ANYTHING THAT FASCINATES YOU; YOU WILL GIVE YOUR TIME AND ATTENTION TO. Positive thoughts will always keep building and feeding on it-self until a negative thought is introduce. If no negative is introduce you will continue along a wonderful positive state of being every day. This would be your reward, the result of maintaining a positive frame of mind every day. This may sound as if it's a lot of work. Yes it takes effort however once you get use to it you will enjoy that way of living so much that you will gladly maintain it. I will remind you that everything and everyone are thoughts manifested in various forms. You; are thought experiencing yourself as a human. You can choose to experience anything any other human has experienced. Do you believe that last statement? If you do then the sky is your limit.

We are all very dependent on our pure positive thoughts for all we want to experience. Sometimes we experience things we don't want to experience this is because of what we think and feel about certain people or thing. Always do your best to keep a pure positive frame of mind about money. Friendship with thought delivers pure positive thoughts, which in turn delivers, happiness, prosperity, joy and well-being. Look forward to tomorrow and all those wonderful thoughts you will experience and things you will do.

The fact that we are all different means that negativity will always exist. However, you do not have to be amongst those people whose thoughts are predominantly negative. You can easily recognise those people by what they say and do. Negative thought has its value. Negative thoughts delivers pain, which tells us that something, is wrong. If you feel that pain, find out what's wrong and fix it as soon as possible. Once you fix it, you free your-self from that pain. If you do not fix it that pain may still be there but you may have gotten used to it. If that pain is in your subconscious it may stop you from doing and having certain things depending on how strong, it is. That pain may manifest itself as fear or anger. If you are aware, that you have any pain about money or anything resolves that pain. Because it may, be your pain that is stopping you from having large sums of money or doing what you, honestly want to do. Yes, pain comes in various forms; some pain come as fear, some as anger, some come as worries and some come as guilt. All reactions are toward people or things, which gives us our experience of that particular person or thing we are reacting too. Remember that a "no" can be a positive reaction as well depending on the situation.

People, react either positively or negatively, your positive reaction towards money will make you feel happy, while your negative reaction will result in pain. We go towards pleasure, happiness and joy, while we do our best to avoid pain. If anyone or anything causes us pain, we will automatically do our best to avoid any such pain. Even, if that action is subconscious action to avoid pain. The same is true with money or anything else so we have to make sure that we have only pure positive thoughts about people and things we want as part of our lives. You may be reacting to money in a negative way without even realising that you are. Notice what you are thinking about money when you think about money. Is it nice, kind friendly thoughts?

If it is negative, you need to change it. You need to be in a state where you do not have any negative thoughts about money. How do you know that you have negative thoughts about money? It's the way you feel when you think about money. If you feel low or fear when you think about money then you need to change your thoughts about money. When you reach a state when you think about money, you feel excited, pleased, secure, happy and comfortable. Money will come knocking on your door. You will have become a true loyal friend of money.

The production of positive doable ideas is the building block for happiness, prosperity and love. Creation of competitive doable ideas results in value for others. This value; is translated in freedom, happiness and prosperity. Creation of positive doable thoughts is essential to happiness and life. Without positive doable thoughts, life would be at a standstill. To prosper you need to own, to have the thoughts and feelings of prosperity in you. You must also be willing to take action, yes to put in the effort accordingly to realize your thoughts and feelings. Sometime we must do things we do not feel like doing even if we know that we should do them. We must find a way of doing them or they will never be done. If you question people you will find that, everyone wants to be happy. However, most of those people do not feel like doing what they know they have to do to get or have certain things. If this is you, you need to create the energy to do. By using Friendship with thought, you will lose all fear to be and do whatever you want and choose. It is essential that you do for yourself what you and you alone can do for you.

Some people rely and wait on others to do for them what they must do for themselves. If you rely on others for your freedom, happiness and prosperity, you will be disappointed. You have to do things to make you happy. If you relinquish responsibility of doing to others what you know you must do for yourself, you are in effect giving over control of you to others. If you give over control of you to others, you will never be happy because only you know at all times what will make you happy. If you hand over control to others for your happiness when you are not happy, you will blame others for your unhappiness.

You and you alone know what you are thinking and how you are feeling. This knowing and feeling of yours puts you in a position to know what you want, only you can know exactly what you want. If you relinquish your responsibility for doing to get what you want people may think and say that you are not worthy of certain things. You are quite capable of thinking and feeling worthy of anything you want. Just as the other person who has things similar to what you want. You are just as worthy to feel happy as the next person. You can be, do and get whatever you need to feel and enjoy your happiness and worthiness.

To have, be or do that which you would like you need the energy to do, the will to do. This energy can only come from you with knowledge of how to create this energy. When you are not afraid, you will do whatever you want to do. Pick, who you want to be or what you want to be and every day "be" that person. That is exactly how you became the person you are today. Only you did it without fully realising what you were doing. You did it unwittingly; nevertheless, you did it. You created the person who you are at the present by the things you thought about and did in the past. Your past is the culmination of you in the present, at this very moment. You can change if you choose to. You can BE the person you want to BE.

If you were wondering, how can you change? This is it. If You Have, Certain Qualities That You Do Not Like You Can Change Them. You Can Take On Any Desirable Qualities You Choose. By changing any of your quality, you change you, you change your identity. For example, if you notice that you are impatient you can develop the quality of patience. You can BE more patient. Use The breath Method to install patient in you.

You may have notice that I have put this secret choice to "be" who you want to "be" under your money. The reason for this is this knowledge is so valuable that people who are interested in money will find it. The second reason is as I have said above that you have to "be" that person. You need to think and feel like the person you want to "be". This is how you make money, by becoming more than you are, by becoming more than a man or a woman. You have to "be" the idea you want to reflect in your life. You have to gradually, live that way. You have to; consciously and deliberately become that person you choose to "be". You must be the idea you want to manifest in your life. You have to live the idea. That means change. The exciting wonderful thing is you see you changing to a better person right in front your eyes. There is nothing, anyone can do about it.

By using the, methods in this book it is like using a map to find your way. It is so much easier when you know where you are going and how to get there. Without this information, people will continue to struggle in the dark.

Remember that you can be anyone you choose to be. I suggest that you choose to "be" someone who is predominantly happy, healthy, rich and wise. Only you can stop your wonderful change, but why would you. Depending on what or who you choose to become time is involved and will vary accordingly. You will not get up one morning and say that you have become a different person without putting in the required time. For example, if you want to be a teacher you must have something to teach. Although you will, find it much easier to teach than the rest. You must do what teachers do to become a teacher. By doing what teachers do you create a teachers identity. Thus, you become a teacher.

If you want to become a millionaire, you need to do what millionaires do. Usually millionaires trade goods or services. So you will need to trade. Eventually you would have created a millionaire identity. The main use of Friendship with thought is to overcome fears. Use the philosophic of Friendship with thought it will help you overcome any fears you may have. Keep in mind that everything you do and have is a representation of your thoughts, including money. Money is one of the greatest thought that humans have ever invented, if not the greatest. Positive thoughts about money are amongst the most valuable and important thoughts humans could have. Thoughts are limitless, thoughts of money cannot run out. It all depends on the individual and what they, habitually think about money. We are drawn; to whatever or whoever gives, us pleasure or make us feel happy.

If you; habitually think happy exciting positive thoughts about money. Any time you think about money or see money you will automatically feel happy and excited. The opposite is also true, anyone or anything that triggers pain in us; we naturally pull away from. However, we create in our lives what we, habitually think about. Even if we do, not want the object of our attention. We will bring it or them into our conscious awareness simply for the fact that we are thinking about it or them. With this realization, with this knowledge what will your habitual predominant thoughts about money be? I recommend only positive thoughts, only happy, joyful pleasant thoughts about your money.

Think about money as a close friend as someone you love, someone you think only pure positive thoughts about. You do not think negative fearful things about your friends. That is why they are your friends. If you did think negative things about those people you would have long ago pulled away from them, they would not still be your friends. So it is with money, get close to money and money will follow you wherever you go. All because of what you habitually think about your friend money. Use The Breath Method to get close to your friend money.

Hold on to a thought by regularly thinking about it and in time you will manifest that thought in your life.

If you want more money, give money your attention and you will be attracted to money. It does not matter where money is you will be attracted to it. It is your natural birthright to live a happy abundant life. However, you must do things to live your life of abundance. By things, I mean the things you really want to do. Remember that it is up to you to "do" whatever you want to do. If one person refuse to help you achieve what you want to achieve try another person. Because of the natural unchangeable law of duality, which states there will always be an opposite. There is always someone, who is willing to help you. Find people who are willing to help you achieve your dreams. When I mention, that there will be people who will help you I am not saying that people will help you for, free.

Remember that people have their responsibility to meet just as you have yours to meet. You may have to pay people to do certain things, which you are not able to do for yourself at present. That being, said there are always those people who are quite willing to, give you a hand up for free. However, you must be willing and be prepared to pay if necessary. By implementing the information contained in these pages, you will easily afford to pay people to help make you money. No one knows everything, no one can be everywhere at the same time. If you knock on one door and it does not open, try another door.

There is always more than one way of achieving the same ends. By using this information, it wouldn't be long before people start opening doors for you. However if you do not put in the necessary effort to achieve your dream, your life will pass by without you having or doing the things you really want. To continually have large sums of money you need to produce competitive value for people. You need to produce things; either goods or services that will make people think and feel happy.

Either consciously or unwittingly, we think what we are worth. We put a value on ourselves as to the things we will do, the possessions we will own and the places we will frequent. Be willing to; honestly say to yourself that you are priceless. That you are worthy to have or do anything you choose because you know your true value. Be willing to say to yourself that you are giving value to the world. Be willing and say to yourself that you are a producer of value to others. When you honestly sat these things, you will find way to do and be what you have said. Be proud of yourself and say that you are a helper you help the world keep going. Yes, you help the world to continue to work. Remember; that it is the individual grain of sand that makes up the beach. You may think that the value you are giving is so small just remember the grain of sand. It is our individual little bits of value we add to the world that makes this world such a wonderful world.

Our thoughts, determines the type of work we will do for a living. The area we will live in and the type of house we will live in. Your thoughts, determines even the type of car you will drive. No one or anything is too good for you unless you think it so.

ANYONE OR ANYTHING IS POSSIBLE FOR YOU IF YOU HABITUALLY THINK THEM SO. It's all a matter of choice, choice of thoughts about you in relation to people and things. As you think you will act, you will behave accordingly. If you think, someone or something is too good for you; you will feel uncomfortable with them. You will do your best not to get too close to that person of thing. On the other hand, if you feel comfortable with someone or something you will draw close to them. You can change the way you think about people and things. When you change your old thoughts about people and things, you will see them in a new light and you will feel different about them.

Continuously think that you can have as much as you want and you will have as much money as you want. Remember that if you are fascinated by anyone or anything that fascination will dominate your life. I am not here saying that you will not care for anyone or anything else. However, that which fascinate you will dominate your life. That which fascinate your life you will give your time and attention too. You can easily, choose something you are happy to be, fascinated by. If you are, fascinated by someone or something you will automatically be attracted to that person or thing. That person or thing will dominate your thoughts; hence, they will dominate your life. Over time you will come to know almost everything about that person or thing, such is the power of fascination. Fascination generates a powerful love that attracts and surpass any mundane. Fascination attracts a mountain of wealth. If these are, what you honestly want be fascinated by money wealth and riches and you will be attracted to them you will give them your time and attention. Treat them with love patience and respect and they will bring happiness into your life.

THOUGHTS WORK

Thought work, everything came about because of thoughts. You can be; one hundred percent absolutely certain of your success because your thought work. The proof that thought works is all around you. The buildings around you are evidence that thought works. Your thought work just as well, the proof of this is you are reading this and understanding it. You are making; sense of it thus proof that your thought works. Any time you eat, have a shower, drive a car, spend money or any other activity is proof that your thought is in perfect working order. Your thought involves everything about you. What you think; what you do and everything else you thought is involved. Your thoughts can work for you or against you. Your positive thoughts will work for you. Your negative thoughts will work against you. Now is the time to let your thoughts work for you to get everything you have ever dreamt, of. To have what you want use your continuous positive thoughts about people and things.

YOUR WONDERFUL MAGICAL GOALS

Use goal setting to have whatever you choose. Write out your goals giving yourself enough time for you to believe that you can have or do what you have written. Write out your goals using only positive words. To let the words that you have written become a part of you read them out aloud to yourself two times a day in the morning and in the evening at your chosen times. As you read them, think and feel happy as if you already have them, because you know for certain, that everything comes from thought. Keep in mind that it is because of thought we have what we have and do what we do. Here are examples of how to write your goals.

It is worth reminding you that you need to, you must, have pure positive thoughts about your goals. Your wonderful thoughts will generate wonderful feelings about your goals.

EXAMPLES OF HOW TO WRITE YOUR GOALS

The Command For Personal Change, Your personal Improvements, Is: I AM

You write this command without a date because personalities changes do not happen suddenly, they do not start and stop on a certain date so you say I AM.

Example: Every day I AM becoming more confident.

Every day I AM becoming more patient.

Every day I AM Thinking and feeling more positive.

The Command For Everything Else Is: I WILL

You write this command with a date in mind because your conscious and subconscious minds need a date to word to-wards.

Remember as you read your command you must feel happy about what you have written.

Assuming it is January 1st 2010

Examples:

BY January 15th 2010, I will open my bank account.

BY July 30th 2010, I will have £5000 in my bank account.

BY December 10th 2012, I will be living in my own five-bedroom house.

By August 15th 2013, I will take the family on a first class holiday to Spain and Portugal.

By December 30th 2015, my net asset will be in excess of one million pounds sterling.

Remember it is always your positive thoughts and feelings that will create the energy and open the way for you to get that sum of money or anything else you want.

Your focus, your predominant positive thoughts should be on the things you choose. It's not about the material things, it's about the energy, it's about the happy thoughts and feelings you put behind the things you want. You; will consciously and subconsciously do happy things to create your goals in your life. They will come, just generate the energy, the feelings, and you will do things to make them manifest.

Your goals will follow they must follow that's the way it works. It is your, positive thoughts and feelings that will create the necessary energy and conditions for you to get your money or anything you choose. You can feel confident you will have what you have chosen because you are the one that generate the needed energy to create your choices in your world. By using, Friendship with thought you will consciously and subconsciously feel happy to do what's necessary to achieve your goals. You will, consciously and subconsciously do things to achieve your goals. Opportunities and situations will present themselves as if by coincidence as if by magic. Those opportunities and situations are not coincidences you have created them by what you have done. When opportunities present themselves as if by magic, take full advantage of them because they are there to present you with what you have commanded them to do.

THE BREATH METHOD

This method is the simplest and one of the most powerful methods in existence to create the feelings of what you have chosen to be part of your life and to program your new personified friends. The method is as simple as breathing itself.

The vast majority of People subconsciously create their world as they have it mainly by complaining and faultfinding. You however are consciously creating your world as you choose it to be. You are creating a wonderful happier world of your own making, your own choice. To do so you must first create qualities such as, confidence, appreciation, happiness, time, doing and love. Link, these powerful thoughts and feelings to you and those people and things you choose as part of your life. Make sure that you do want those people and things in your life because you will pull them into your life.

The people and things you want in your life should make you feel happy. You like you even more especially when you make you feel happy. Your happiness is your natural birthright.

I will remind you that every single thing you do has an element of time, yes time is involve in all we do. Keep in mind to create anything you must first think about it and pay for it with your thought and feeling which involves you paying attention to it.

Your thought should create wonderful feeling about the object of your attention. It is this feeling, which is the energy that will create and attach you emotionally to the objects and situations you choose to be in your world.

If you have ever went through a divorce or have been in a close friendship that has ended, at the time of the end you felt emotionally as if you were being tear apart. That was your emotional links you previously formed being, disconnected. That state also accurse in varying intensity with pets or any material thing with which people had formed an emotional link.

YOUR INSTALLATION. THIS IS WHAT YOU DO: close your mouth and breathing in slowly only through your nose. As you breathe in through your nose and with a lovely smile on your face, say the name of the person, quality or thing you choose softly in your mind. At the same time feel that wonderful happy feeling of how it feels to have that person, quality or thing as part of your life. Now with your mouth firmly still close and breathing out only through your nose say the name of the person or the quality you choose in your life.

As you breathe in hold that thought and feeling inside of you for 10 seconds so it will transform your life. Now consciously and subconsciously you know you have that thought of the person, thing or quality living inside of you. You can now say you have the thought of that person, thing or quality inside of you.

Now all you have to do is keep on feeding those thoughts and they will grow. Your subconscious does not question your actions. The next time you use this method no need to hold your breath for ten seconds. You only have to hold it for 10 seconds once, each time you use a different word or quality.

Here it is again.

Now with your mouth firmly close and with a wonderful smile on your face you breathe in slowly only through your nose, saying softly the name of the person or quality you choose as part of your life. At the same time feel that wonderful happy feeling of having that person, thing or quality as part of your life.

As you breathe out slowly through your nose only, with that wonderful smile on your face, say softly in your mind the name of that person or thing and feel that wonderful happy feeling of having that person, quality or thing in your life.

You can use this method anywhere anytime you please day or night. The more you use it; it is the quicker you will become a friend of that person thing or quality. Hence, the sooner you will have them in your world, as part of your life.

This method applies to anything, absolutely anything. If it is a human, you chose, as part of your life. That human would, have to happily want to be part of your life. Chances are they will want to because of the lovely type of person you are becoming, the more wonderful type of person you are changing into.

Knowing that you have the thought and feeling of them already alive in you assures you that you are on your way to having them as part of your life.

Keep in mind that the thought of the person or thing must come first so make the thought of what you choose part of your life first.

Keep doing this creative action regularly and you will soon feel that, that person or thing is part of your life, they will manifest in your world.

When you think of them, your thought will trigger your wonderful feeling of them. Carry on doing it long enough so it will become a part of you and transform your life. The people and things will come into your life as if by coincidence, as if by magic. I repeat those people and things should make you feel happy when you think of them that is why you have chosen them to be in your life, because they will come into your life.

As I said, you can do this creation and programming anywhere at any time. You can also do this creation and programming while relaxing with your eyes close. Obviously, you would not close your eyes if you were in a potential dangerous situation. Think and see that person or thing and feel that wonderful feeling of having that person or thing in your world.

This is the method of how you emotionally link, program, attract, attach and make people and things parts of your life. By creating and linking a wonderful emotional feeling of them in your thought, you are automatically creating them in objective reality in your world. By repeating this method you are subconsciously programming your thought, you are connecting those people, qualities or things to you.

You may have noticed that there is no date to this method that is because this is not goal setting. With goal, setting your subconscious mind needs a date by which it will achieve a certain objective. Once again I will remind you that our field of focus our attention, our thought determine what we have in life. As you change, keep your thoughts on the people and things you choose to be in your world and you will have them as part of your life.

When you are ready do something special to mark you dedication to a better way of life, a more happy and prosperous way of life. Treat yourself. Set a date and treat yourself. You are worth it; forget how expensive it is. Do something that the person you are becoming will find normal and exciting to do. If you want to be rich, happy, and powerful or anything else, success comes from taking action, success comes from getting started. Take a step by doing something in line with what you want to accomplish.

YOUR HAPPY COMMISSION

Happiness does not come about by chance. Happiness is not automatic. We have to do things to make us feel happy. We have to do things to create happiness. To be happy we must display certain positive habitual positive qualities. To be predominantly happy we must put into practice certain positive qualities. To be happy we need to develop and display certain positive attitude. To be happy you need to display predominantly positive qualities. Here are some qualities that all successful people use: confidence, powerful, caring, happy, generous, peaceful, grateful, healthy, positive, balance, lucky, helpful, lovely, wonderful, nice, friendly, calm, relax, easygoing, gentle, studious, and wealthy. This list could go on. Find more of these types of positive qualities and add them not only to the list but also to yourself.

As you keep on growing you will add to the list and display these positive qualities in your everyday life. You will feel and see the wonderful results of these qualities in your life. Continue to reinforce these qualities until they are, deeply ingrained in you. Let them become parts of you and you will be exactly as they describe you. You are now ready to live the life you have always wanted to live. You are now ready to; continually use your new personality and new attitude to do whatever makes you happy. You are now ready to; continually develop your new self-image. Remember that your self-esteem has no limit. You are unique and priceless to you. What others think, about you that is their thought, they are entitled to their opinions just as you are to yours. Nothing or anyone is too good for you; you are worth it, whatever it may be.

The fact that, you are priceless and worth it mean that you deserve anything you want and choose by going for it. If you go for it, you deserve to have the experience of it. If you make up excuses why you can't do something those excuses will keep you from doing it. It is only when we tell our self that we can't do something we don't do what we need to do. What you are really saying to your self is excuse me from doing it. By making up excuse, people are justifying themselves or exempting themselves from taking needed action. To have whatever you want you must take action. Using the methods and knowledge you have discovered in these pages will help to make you taking action much easier. Keep on using the information in these pages and you will notice that your fears of taking action will fade and disappear. Realize that it is only what you are thinking that is stopping you from taking action to realize your dreams. You can just as easily think positive things to help you to take action towards your dreams.

We as humans generate electromagnetic energy to the universe. When you think of certain people or things, you generate a certain type of energy.

You experience this energy as feelings as it leaves you. You generate two types of energy. You either generate positive or negative energy to the universe. These two types of energy keep the universe in balance. There will be people who will be generating predominantly negative energy. There will also be people who will generate predominately-positive energy to the universe. What type of energy you generate is largely a matter of choice. When you feel happy, joyful, wonderful, marvellous or any other feel good feeling, you are generating positive energy to the universe. When you are feeling angry, frustrated, low or afraid you are generating negative energy to the universe.

You can choose what type of energy you want to, predominantly generate. Positive energy makes you feel happy and negative energy makes you feel sad. Positive energy vibrates at a high frequency. Negative energy vibrates at a low frequency. You feel these energy vibrations as feelings. Have; you ever heard someone say that they are feeling low? It is because of the way they are vibrating, the type of energy they are generating. The low vibrations, is what is making them feel the way they are feeling. High frequency vibrations make us feel good, happy. Usually people generate these feelings naturally, when they accomplish something wonderful. Like passing your exam or passing your driving test or getting engage or married.

People also generate these types of feeling under the influence of alcohol or drugs. There could be a problem with drugs or alcohol in that they have painful side effects, hang over's. They could also become painful additive, habits that lead to all sorts of problems. There will always be people generating one type of energy or another. Generating positive energy naturally is pain free and life inducing.

To that purpose, your commission awaits you. On the next page, you will find your commission and an oath. If you decide to generate predominantly positive happy energy to the universe, take your oath. By taking your oath, you will have done one of the most important things for the rest of your life. You will have decided to be predominantly happy, healthy, joyful and wealthy. Because these will, be the results of your new mentality, your new personality, your new attitude. By signing the contract and taking your oath. You are demonstrating your commitment to yourself to change your life through positive thoughts. While you continue to follow the path of positivity with confidence, determination and fearless courage. Remember that you are part of the universe and are worth to share in the wealth of the universe.

YOUR PRICELESS CONTRACT

This is an example of your oath: I Ronnie Jerome Dufeal Now today on the 16th December 2009 hereby takes up my commission to continually, generate feel-good energy to the universe for the rest of my life to the best of my potential.

Feel in the space in your contract below with your own name and the current date and year.

Now put your hand on your heart and take the oath by reading it out aloud to yourself.

I------------------------------ Now on the---------hereby takes up my commission to continually, generate feel-good energy to the universe for the rest of my life to the best of my potential.

Your signature---

Welcome to your new life. You are now on the side of the universe that generates predominantly positive feel-good energy. By accepting your commission and taking your oath, you have chosen to be a predominant positive part of the universe. Your contract is like a partnership with the universe.

In fact, it is a partnership with the universe so take your oath to heart and do everything in your power to keep your part of the relationship alive by you feeling good as much as your thoughts will remind you.

People like you because of the way you make them feel. Make as much people as you can happy along your journey of life. It's not only they will like you for making them happy but because you will make yourself happy in the process of making others happy.

A WONDERFUL CONCLUSION

For many years, before I discovered Friendship with thought I truly struggled in every single area of my life on this planet we call home. Using Friendship with thought most of my fears are no longer fears but thoughts I need to recognize as only thoughts. My sincere wish for you is that you will understand most of what you have read and most importantly decide to try it, yes use it. You can only become a better, more successful, more wealth person if you do. By using it, you will experience a life of unlimited opportunities and infinite possibilities because thought has the power to give you exactly what you want. In order to want something you must first think about it. Then you will manifest it in objective reality. If you do not understand certain points talk about it, ask questions about it. As long as you do not give up when you ask questions, you will find the answers, this I promise you. All the answers are available you just have not discovered them yet.

If you decide to use this, wonderful gift that has been pass on to you, you will be transform beyond recognition from your old limiting personality and attitudes. You will change to a confident, secure, happy wealthy person by making Friendship with thought your way of life. Friendship with thought is more than an education it is a transformation.

You are unique and very fortunate; out of billions of humans today, you have this knowledge in your possession. Very few people will have this knowledge when compared with earth's population. Now that you have the master key use it to enter any door, you choose.

Use it to take control of your thought in any situation. Use it to create your wonderful world as you choose. Use it to enter the world of the rich and stay there if that is your choice. Use it to go through life first class. Now that you know the power, make it your own and uses it to do and have whatever you choose. Remember what Friendship with thought is and you will automatically remember that you have the master key. I wish you well in your new life and I know with absolute certainty that you will be all right, as you continue to live your life with Friendship with thought.

FOR MORE VISIT

www.dufealcontinuous.co.uk